Pastoral Marital Therapy

Integration Books

STUDIES IN PASTORAL PSYCHOLOGY,
THEOLOGY, AND SPIRITUALITY

Robert J. Wicks,
General Editor

also in this series

Clinical Handbook of Pastoral Counseling
R. Wicks, R. Parsons, and D. Capps (Eds.)
Adolescents in Turmoil,
Parents Under Stress
by Richard D. Parsons

Pastoral Marital Therapy

A Practical Primer
for Ministry to Couples

Stephen Treat
and
Larry Hof

Integration Books

paulist press / new york / mahwah

Library of Congress Cataloging-in-Publication Data

Treat, Stephen R., 1951-
    Pastoral marital therapy.

    (Integration books)
    Includes bibliographies.
    1. Marriage counseling.   2. Pastoral counseling.
3. Marriage—Religious aspects—Christianity.
I. Hof, Larry.   II. Title.   III. Series.
BV4012.2.T74   1987   253.5   87-6048
ISBN 0-8091-2889-6 (pbk.)

Published by Paulist Press
997 Macarthur Boulevard
Mahwah, New Jersey 07430

Printed and bound in the
United States of America

Contents

Foreword

Persons in pastoral roles are frequently confronted with the issues, problems, challenges, and questions that arise in Christian marriages. Yet, Christian laity, clergy and religious often feel—and are—unprepared to respond. Therefore, the anxiety couples bring with them is often met with a similar anxiety on the ministers' part. In such circumstances those in ministry often ask themselves: "How can I possibly sufficiently understand, apply and balance—much less integrate—the theology and psychology of marriage to help this couple in need?"

With this question as a backdrop, Stephen Treat and Larry Hof have addressed the need for essential theory and skills in their practical primer for ministry to couples. Moreover, unlike other treatments of the topic which emphasize psychology and only pay lip service to theology, Treat and Hof—who have credentials and experience both in ministry and marital counseling—have developed a book which is thoroughly integrated.

Their volume provides theory and technique in a way that proves a little bit of knowledge does *not* have to be a dangerous thing. They note both the treatment limitations of the person in ministry who has not received specialized advanced education in pastoral counseling or psychology and discuss the need to appreciate when and how to refer to a mental health professional. However, within the framework of this book, they also provide a clear and practical approach to understanding and intervening with couples who come for assistance. This approach enables ministers to gain clarity and improved abilities in problem solving within their relationship.

In their efforts to demonstrate how a person in ministry can be helpful, they point out the uniqueness of pastoral marital counseling/ therapy. It comes through in their use of biblical themes, a presentation of how sacred Scriptures can be understood and applied, and an appreciation of the special role of ethics and moral principles in facilitating communication between spouses.

Through the use of illustrations and the coverage of conceptual cornerstones of marital counseling, they bring to life relevant treatment approaches from the wealth and maze of material that is available in the literature today. Topics include: treatment boundaries and limits, setting and fees, marital myths, contracting for change, the need for balance in a relationship, defenses and expectations, the importance and difficulty of listening, individual development and personality styles, communication and conflict management skills, the extended family, the formulation of a treatment plan, sexuality, and other issues and concerns unique to the marital setting that come out of their experience.

Although this primer is clearly intended to enable persons in ministry to provide limited help to couples, its content should provide an incentive to those who deal with marital issues to read further and seek additional opportunities for education in the area. The strength in this book is that it reminds us that to attempt to do pastoral marital counseling requires preparation. It gives solid information so that we don't turn away those who ask for support and some initial assistance in understanding and problem solving. Yet, it also explicitly and implicitly reminds us that to reach out to others by attempting to do *in depth* marital therapy without both a strong theological base and psychological understanding of marital counseling is dangerous. The availability of such realistic, hopeful and helpful information for assisting Christian couples in their attempt to deal with the stresses of commitment and personal development in an anxious and fragmented world is more important now than ever before.

Robert J. Wicks
Series Editor

Introduction

The theological foundations for the institution of marriage have been described in books and articles of every religious denomination. The psychological foundations have also been the subject of prolific writing by authors representing virtually every psychological school. However, attempts to create an integrated, theologically based and psychologically sound approach to marriage and marital therapy are still in the infancy stage of development. Some theologians write about the role of the pastoral therapist as one of holding or "saving" the marriage at all costs. Others believe that divorce is a sin, or that the dominance of males over females is scripturally based and morally correct. Theological writers on marriage and marital therapy often describe in great detail the role of love and caring between husband and wife, without addressing the complexities of what truly enables a person to be able to fully love his/her partner. On the other hand, many so-called pastoral counselors and marital therapists speak to various marital issues without a strong background in current theory relating to marital dynamics and with only a cursory nod to the need to integrate their theology with therapeutic approach.

An integrated and current theological and psychological approach which speaks to the development and enhancement of the psychologically healthy and spiritually rich individual and marital couple is needed. How else can pastors begin to develop the integrated skills needed to fulfill two roles they are so often called upon to play together, the role of pastor and the role of counselor/therapist? In the complex society in which we live, it is crucial that every pastor have some abilities and skills in each of these areas, if only to make an intelligent referral and to offer genuine and empathic support to individuals and couples who are experiencing marital problems. In an attempt to address such a need, this primer will outline a theological basis for a Christian marriage with implications for the pastoral marital therapist (Chapter 1), possibilities and limitations of

3

the practice of pastoral marital therapy within the context of the local church (Chapter 2), and psychological foundations, approaches, and techniques needed to be an effective pastoral marital therapist from a sound systemic orientation and essentially Christian perspective (Chapters 3–6).

The discussion on marital therapy will include couples and individuals who come to counseling for insight and alleviation of difficulties experienced in a marital or committed relationship. Marital or dyadic therapy focuses on the systemic relationship and includes examination of individual psychopathology and family of origin in the context of the marital system. The terms "pastoral therapist" and "pastoral counselor" will be used interchangeably.

Chapter 1

A Theology of Marriage for the Pastoral Marital Therapist

In the field of pastoral marital therapy there are often two types of clinicians. One type began their training in a theological discipline but devalued theological principles and beliefs for secular psychological understandings and clinical techniques. The second type had a similar theological background but never sought a psychological education. The latter group's goal in "counseling" parishioners would be to communicate clearer biblical understandings, and areas in which their clients were confused or fallen into sin.

Neither of the above perspectives of pastoral marital counseling is adequate or appropriate for the care of souls or the healing of relationships. To be a pastoral marital therapist without a personal belief and commitment to the Lord or without an ability to integrate theological concepts and the Holy Spirit into the therapeutic sessions is a misnomer. Such an individual should be called a marital therapist, not a pastoral marital therapist. However, to consider oneself a marital therapist without an in-depth psychological and systemic background is unethical and dangerous for clients. A great deal of harm and hurt has been created by the well-meaning pastor or lay leader who intervenes without basic understanding.

The Holy Spirit and the reconciling power of Jesus Christ need to be as powerfully applied in a therapeutic session as the systemic concepts provided by psychology. When such an integration takes place the uniqueness and power of the pastoral marital therapist becomes evident. In the following discussion an integration of theology and systemic principles is begun.

Christian Marriage
A Spiritual, Growthful Vessel

What a sad time in the life of the twelve disciples when they understood that Jesus was foretelling his crucifixion and death. They had grown to depend on Jesus' direction and teaching, and many were insecure as to which course to follow. Jesus understood their despair and the insecurities of their faith. He consoled his followers by promising to send the Paraclete, the Helper, the Holy Spirit who was to complete the work that he had already begun. Jesus said, "I will ask the Father and he will give you another Counselor to be with you forever, even the Spirit of truth whom the world cannot receive, because it neither sees him nor knows him; you know him, for he dwells with you, and he will be within you. . . . The Counselor, the Holy Spirit, whom the Father will send in my name, he will teach you all things and bring to your remembrance all that I have said to you" (Jn 14:15, 25). Jesus sends the Holy Spirit, as he did some two thousand years ago, to lead people into truth and understanding. This search for truth and understanding, guided by the Holy Spirit, is the pathway to the kingdom of God and a primary goal for the pastoral marital therapist. But where is the kingdom of God, and where does the Holy Spirit lead each individual? Jesus said that the kingdom of God is within each person, "The kingdom of God is within you" (Lk 17:21). The context for the work of the Holy Spirit and the search for truth is an exploration within oneself, the search for self-understanding, to discover, even if only in part, how one is created in God's image. The "healthy" marriage then becomes one in which two people follow the guidance of the Holy Spirit and constantly attempt to discover truth and understanding within the self and especially as it unfolds in the complexities of an intimate relationship.

What moves a person closer to truth and understanding? Which aspects of truth and understanding allow a person to be a healthier individual and more loving partner? Being led by the Holy Spirit into truth and understanding will be defined in this primer as an inward search for self-understanding, self-responsibility and wholeness. The self is defined by the authors as all of the parts and aspects of character and personality, both innate and socially learned, which make up the whole person. "This innate striving for wholeness is the de-

cisive factor in any real understanding of the process whereby healing is brought about by consciousness" (Phillips, 1948, p. 31). The
striving for self-understanding becomes the means to discovering the
kingdom of God, and by definition needs to be one of the highest, if
not the highest, priority of a Christian. "There is in man a longing
and tendency for wholeness. . . . This wholeness can only be
achieved through knowledge of the missing part, that is, when man
has become fully conscious" (Phillips, 1948, p. 30). The missing part
is often unconscious and frequently represented as an aspect of personality in the chosen marital partner, i.e., an extrovert might marry
an introvert or an intellectual might seek out a more emotional partner. The old maxim that "opposites attract" is often true and based
in a desire by an individual to be whole. A sense of individual wholeness can be achieved within a marriage when each partner is able to
learn from and adopt the strengths of the other. Unfortunately, this
search for truth and wholeness is often neglected and even devalued
by the individual who, instead, seeks perfection and purity as his/
her/their Christian goal. In such a case the missing part unconsciously sought after in a partner becomes a source of anger and division instead of reconciliation. "Salvation never means the complete
destruction of creatureliness and absorption into the divine . . . the
self, even in the highest reaches of its consciousness, is still the finite
self which must regard the pretensions of universality as a sin" (Niebuhr, 1941, p. 170). Healthier than the search for perfection is the goal
of being a peacemaker. Integration of Jesus' words "Blessed are the
peacemakers" necessitates an inward search for peace among all of
the unpleasant memories and warring factions of the self. Having discovered an increasing sense of peace within oneself, a person can
share love and affection with one's marital partner in increasingly
more creative and patient ways. The pathways to such peace are
found both in the scriptural passages which lead the individual into
a more complete self-understanding and wholeness, and in the marital relationship when respect, sensitivity, and desire allow for personal awareness and integration. Such consciousness is at the heart
of Christian theology and Christian marriage. "The greatest ethical
value, according to Jesus, is to become a conscious person, and this
means being a free person" (Sanford, 1974, p. 28). As two individuals
are enabled to be conscious and free in the context of a committed

relationship, the deep potential of Christian marriage can be ful-
filled.

Marriage is the joining and working together of two individuals.
On the specific topic of marriage Jesus had relatively little to say. His
emphasis was primarily on the spiritual growth and well-being of the
individual. The contention of the authors is that to the extent that
each individual applies his/her faith to the inward search for truth
and understanding, the marriage of these individuals has the potential to be a spiritual and growthful vessel. Two people who deny their
inward journey block the essential work of the Holy Spirit, preventing movement toward the kingdom of God and the realization of the
full potential of Christian marriage.

Even though Jesus shared few teachings on the institution of
marriage, every passage which enlightens self-understanding is a
cornerstone for Christian marriage and for the approach of the pastoral marital therapist. Jesus felt so strongly about the work of the
Holy Spirit that he made violation or ignoring of the "work" the only
sin that cannot be forgiven: "Therefore I tell you, every sin and blasphemy will be forgiven but the blasphemy against the Holy Spirit
will not be forgiven. And whoever says a word against the Son of Man
will be forgiven but whoever speaks against the Holy Spirit will not
be forgiven" (Mt 12:31). It is similarly true psychologically that individuals who refuse to search for self-understanding often experience confusion, helplessness, and a lack of personal balance or
integration. Blocking the work of the Holy Spirit often results in individual suffering, marital despair, and the failure to discover truth
and wholeness intrapsychically and interpersonally. Classically, a
presenting couple for marital therapy will not be searching for self-
understanding, but instead to convince the pastoral therapist of the
correctness of each of their perspectives. Their judgment and blame
thwart reconciliation and the work of the Holy Spirit.

There are many guideposts offered by the Scriptures which, if
understood in a marital context, would lead a person closer to following the path of the Holy Spirit toward the kingdom of God. Each
guidepost speaks to the growth of a healthy individual from a Christian perspective. A Christian marriage is one in which two people
are seeking such health, individually and together. In the following
scriptural passages, several theological underpinnings for marriage

and the practice of pastoral marital therapy are discussed. The scriptural passages chosen focus on (1) loving and reconciling aspects of the self, (2) judging and blaming between spouses, (3) feelings of superiority and inferiority in marital relationships, (4) marital process considerations as more important than content, (5) formation of boundaries for marital satisfaction, and (6) "reconciling oneself" to marriage.

Guideposts for Growth

1. Loving and Reconciling Aspects of the Self

"Love your enemies, do good to them which hate you" (Lk 6:27).

This Scripture reference, in part, speaks to rules of interrelationships, the manner in which one person is supposed to treat another. Another possible interpretation is an individualistic one, in which the enemy that needs to be loved is the darker side of the self, i.e., all those characteristics and experiences of personality which the individual finds difficult to look at or accept. The "enemy" for many is being perceived as, or perceiving oneself as, being meek, weak, ignorant, aggressive, impotent, lustful, etc. These aspects of personality gain power over a person when the individual does not recognize them or accept them as part of the self. If an individual is able to love or accept these "enemies" within himself/herself it is not difficult to accept the same traits when seen in one's spouse. If the "enemy" cannot be loved, some hatred or disdain of oneself and one's spouse will probably prevail. In a marriage a husband might report to the therapist that he feels that his wife is incompetent. The pastoral therapist will most likely need to confront the husband to understand the fear of his own incompetence which he projects onto his wife. Conversely, a wife might state that her husband is powerful and domineering, while not understanding the domineering and powerful aspects of her personality.

On a societal plane, a classic example of the above is found in prejudicial thought. Prejudice is most often based in the inability of an individual to love some aspect of the "darker" side of himself/herself. Instead of accepting one's feelings of ignorance or impotence, for example, a person projects them onto others. A prejudiced person, as we all are to some degree, then feels superior to the people he/she believes are demonstrating these ignorant or impotent behaviors. For example, the prejudice that all black men are lazy may come from a person's inability to look at and accept his/her own laziness.

Further ramifications for marriage are clear. Marriages often consist of a whole series of projections from one spouse onto the other. Instead of loving one's internal "enemy" a spouse will judge the partner for the same qualities which the spouse refuses to examine within himself/herself. Such a couple will come to therapy and begin by judging and blaming each other for the marital difficulties being experienced.

Consider the following: A husband openly criticizes his wife for being dependent on others. In truth, he fears his own dependency needs. A wife criticizes her husband for being passive or dependent when she is fearful of her own passivity and dependent personality. Others criticize the "dominance" of a partner, when, in part, they are fearful of their own power and assertiveness.

Other examples of refusal to love a part of the self appear in couples in which one person protects his or her spouse. This person senses the fragility of the partner and protects him/her from having to look at the fearful part. For example, a woman presents in therapy her concerns about the hostility and depression she sometimes feels. When both the husband and the wife are seen in therapy, the husband also agrees that his wife has a problem. In fact, the husband was obsessively rigid, denying much of his own hurt and anger. The wife, in order to protect the husband from having to look at his hostility and fragility, attempted to become the focus for treatment. When this couple came to therapy she could not understand why she was so hostile. He wanted to "assist" the therapist in helping his wife figure it out.

The pastoral marital therapist needs to begin theoretically with an understanding of how individuals fear and refuse to integrate certain emotions, personality traits, or experiences deemed fearful or repulsive. If such parts are not integrated within the individual, they are often projected and reacted to within the marriage. Revenge is frequently the outcome.

> "You have heard that it was said, an eye for an eye and a tooth for a tooth. But now I tell you, do not take revenge on someone who does you wrong. If anyone slaps you on the right cheek, let him slap you on your left too" (Mt 5:38).

For the individual, taking revenge is a form of self-hatred and/ or lack of self-understanding. Revenge is most often an angry statement in which a person wants to get back at someone else for some perceived wrong that has been perpetrated. The presupposition of most revengeful acts is that the wronged party was a victim and had little or nothing to do with the incident of perceived wrongdoing. Of course, there are singular examples in which this might be the case, but in many if not most situations both parties contributed to the problem. It is a more powerful position for an individual to attempt to understand what allowed him/her to be taken advantage of or hurt in the first place. In the process of revenge, a person does not look at his/her own complicity but projects it onto another or hides from it by making someone else the villain.

Revenge is a very common dynamic in marriage. Instead of applying self-understanding to the reasons why a hurt or difficulty continues, a spouse feels like a victim and seeks to hurt the other person. In revengeful situations, the couple's negative communication often escalates and both partners become less able to objectively and caringly look at what they are contributing to the problem. For instance, when one partner has an affair, the "innocent" partner often wants to take revenge. The "innocent" party might decide to have an affair, tell all the church friends, or perhaps even file for divorce. Such revenge blinds the "innocent" party from understanding what dynamics within the marriage contributed to the affair and how he/ she might have contributed to these dynamics. It is easier to look at one part of behavior (the affair), one person (the partner), and one sin (infidelity), than it is to look at a complex system composed of multiple, interacting and reciprocal behaviors, issues, feelings, persons, and sins. It is easier to take revenge than to look at one's own complicity in whatever the marital difficulty is! The pastor without training in systems theory might have the following discussion with a couple after the discovery of an affair.

Wife — Thank you for seeing us, pastor. Our marriage is having a very rough time.
Pastor — What seems to be the problem?
Wife — My husband had an affair. I caught him the other night with another woman.
Pastor — (to the husband) How do you explain this?
Husband — I don't know what happened. I have been really unhappy in the marriage and things got out of hand.
Pastor — Do you understand that this is no excuse?
Wife — What should we do now?
Pastor — Let's see if we can get your husband some help.

This condensed dialogue is common and illustrative of a theologically and systemically inappropriate approach damaging to all parties concerned. Both the husband and the wife in the above example should be in treatment together to determine what caused the affair in their marriage.

The pastoral marital therapist should stop vengeful or vitriolic behavior and encourage shared responsibility. He/she needs to approach a couple with the understanding that each of their self-concepts and levels of self-love affects their ability to love the other.

"You shall love your neighbor as yourself" (Mt 19:19).

This passage of Scripture is often read as a command from Jesus as to how a person should act toward another. A further insight into the meaning of the passage is best understood through the words "as yourself." In relationships, the degree to which you love yourself is or "shall" be about the degree you can love another. Furthermore, those parts of the self that are difficult to love or accept are frequently the exact qualities which a person rejects in another.

The implications for a marriage are widespread. The spouse who has low self-regard will often believe the partner to be unworthy. A spouse who feels incompetent may become angry at the perceived incompetence of the marital partner. Such examples are numerous, and all contain a common theme: the inability to love certain parts of the self makes it difficult to love those same parts in someone else.

The role of the pastoral marital therapist is to help each individual of the dyad come to terms with the shadow side of the self. This shadow side, the weaknesses and fearful aspects of personality, often appears more quickly and can be more readily assessed within the intimate relationship of a marriage. It is often in marriage that the fears and anxieties produced by the power of the shadow side cannot be adequately defended against. The result is projection of responsibility, sometimes regressive behavior, and distancing to ward off fears of vulnerability. For example, a woman did not feel she was worthy of love and caring. Consequently, whenever her husband tried to care he was rebuffed or it simply was not noticed. In a complementary way the husband was fearful of rejection and suffered from low self-esteem. He was convinced that his wife constantly rejected him. The fears of both spouses prevented a natural healing process within the marriage.

However, marriage also provides a wonderful opportunity for healing and reconciliation within and between people. If a spouse can learn about himself/herself and find acceptance from a loving partner, a new spiritual beginning emerges. The role of the pastoral marital therapist is to create a non-judgmental environment in which the projections can be taken back to oneself and used for self-understanding, where both partners can learn to love more aspects of themselves so that each, in turn, can love the other more completely.

2. Judging and Blaming Between Partners

> "Whichever one of you who has committed no sin may throw the first stone at her" (*Good News Bible:* Jn 8:7).

The pastoral marital therapist needs to recognize, point out, and stop the cycle of one spouse projecting responsibility onto another with the consequent blaming and defensive or attacking reactions. Modeling after Christ, the therapist should ask each individual to start the search for understanding and resolution of the difficulties, by looking at one's own behavior. Through the projection of responsibility onto one's partner, an inward search for understanding is blocked. Accepting part of the responsibility ("part," because to accept all of the responsibility might limit the potential for someone else to see his/her culpability) often begins the process of self-understanding and movement toward the kingdom of God. Too often, "Man is tempted by the basic insecurity of human existence to make himself doubly secure" (Niebuhr, 1941). A spouse often attains this security when he/she gives, or the partner accepts, all of the responsibility for a marital problem, or all of the responsibility for a marital success.

Two of the fundamental ways of thinking about human relationships are called linear thinking and systemic thinking. A linear thinker believes that relational dynamics happen by cause and effect. Find the cause and you can understand and change the effect. If there is a problem some "one" person must be at fault. A systemic thinker believes in circular patterns of responsibility and causality, tending to examine the contribution every person is making to marital harmony or disharmony. If there is a difficulty in a marriage, both partners are somehow involved in it, and should take part of the responsibility for the remedy. Differentiating linear and systemic thinking is sometimes difficult. For further clarification consider the following: A husband comes home late from work and his wife responds by being upset and angry. A linear thinker might say that the problem, in this case, is that the husband needs to learn how to budget his time better so that he arrives home on time. He is the person responsible for the problem. A systemic thinker would recognize the circular nature of the difficulty. The husband might be coming home late because his wife is often upset and angry and the wife might be upset and angry because the husband is often showing irresponsibility by, for instance, coming home late. While this situation, somewhere in history, did have a beginning, a cause, it rarely can be accurately described and becomes a problem in marital relationships of "the chicken or the egg." Many times there are two traceable "beginnings" somewhere in the life of each partner, even before they met each other! A systems oriented therapist would be less concerned with the origin of the difficulty, than with what each partner is doing to contribute to and perpetuate it.

When Jesus said, "Let him who is without sin cast the first stone," he was describing the Christian relationship in a more systemic than linear way. With relatively few exceptions, couples who present their issues in marital therapy are looking for cause outside of the self and have forgotten to look at their own sin. Each partner might secretly say, "If the pastor could only get my partner to see what he/she is doing wrong everything would be all right."

The difficulties with projecting sin or responsibility onto one's partner are many. Of these difficulties, perhaps the most debilitating one is that rendering responsibility outside of the self creates feelings of powerlessness within the self. The partner who is projecting blame is placing responsibility upon the one person whom he/she has little ability to affect. It feels very powerless to try to force another person to grow. Healthful growth and acceptance of responsibility are ultimately controlled internally. A spouse who attempts to change a partner will often experience frustration and foment resistance.

A pastoral marital therapist, working from a Christian perspective, desires that each person become more powerful through the journey of self-understanding. Through this journey, a person becomes very powerful because he/she will be able to change his/her own behavior and will not have to exclusively rely on the movement of his/her partner. Judgment of another's lack of movement is powerless behavior and will only deepen the destructive cycle of communication.

> "Judge not, and you will not be judged . . . for the measure you give will be the measure you get back" (Lk 6:37).

As has been stressed, Jesus was interested in helping each individual pull back the projection of responsibility onto another person. What is significant about this passage of Scripture, in comparison to the passages on "sin" or the "log and speck," is the additional concept that projecting blame onto another is reciprocal in nature. That is, judging others does not merely hurt the other person, but also hurts, in a similar manner, the person doing the judging. For example, a wife judges her husband for being distant and cold. The more she judges the more he becomes distant and unresponsive, leaving the wife alone (distant) and feeling unloved (cold).

Her judgments toward her husband became the experienced reality
for herself, as Jesus suggested that they would be when he said "in
the same way." If a spouse judges his/her partner for being unloving,
uncaring, removed, angry, etc., he/she will most likely receive the
same treatment and feel the same way, without realizing how his/her
own judging and reacting contribute to the ongoing nature of the
problem.

In pastoral marital therapy, once the cycles of blame can be
stopped, a couple is ready to begin the search within themselves using the Holy Spirit as their guide. Unfortunately, stopping such
cycles of blame is often difficult for pastors or lay leaders. Pastoral
therapists who are soft-spoken or fearful of anger and confrontation
often don't allow a couple to truly address the emotional issues which
each partner feels. By intellectualizing and controlling the therapeutic session the pastor can suppress the true emotions of the couple,
and the cyclical nature of these emotions will not be revealed or
worked with in the session. The pastoral marital therapist must be
comfortable and confident enough to allow the couple to share hurt
and frustration, and skilled enough to redirect and reframe it. When
this is done the responsibility for the health of the marriage rests
upon each individual, and there will be some power within each person to affect change. Such a marriage becomes an arena where love
is more fully understood and personal growth is available to both
partners. At this time intimacy between the two partners is a real
possibility.

3. Feelings of Superiority and Inferiority in Marital Relationships

"Blessed are the meek; for they shall inherit the earth" (Mt
5:5).

During Jesus' earthly journeys, as today, most people attempt
to hide the fact that they feel, in part, meek or inferior. The hiding
can take the form of trying to be superior. "The fact that human am-
bitions know no limits must therefore be attributed not merely to the
infinite capacities of the human imagination, but to an uneasy recognition of man's finiteness, weakness and dependence which becomes more apparent the more we seek to obscure them" (Niebuhr,

1941). A person striving for power in marriage or notoriety in society can do so at the expense of understanding his/her own fragilities and meekness. An understanding of Jesus' calling the meek "blessed" can correct this imbalance.

For the individual, honoring meekness means that he/she does not have to suppress the gentle, passive, and weak parts of the self. For the Christian marriage, honoring meekness means that a spouse will not be frightened by, or take advantage of, his/her partner's more fragile qualities.

Furthermore, tradition has dictated that being meek is a quality of personality which more fits into the definition of what it means to be feminine rather than masculine. This attribution has limited both men and women, and decreased the potentialities for the institution of marriage to be a center for personal growth and wholeness. Women have often been devalued because meekness, and its aspects of compassion, sensitivity, and vulnerability, are secondary characteristics in a society which more often than not rewards power and autonomy. Some women have hidden from their own feared power behind a culturally scripted mask of "meekness" or feelings of inferiority. Men are also devalued because the strived for image of power and autonomy limits their ability to relate compassionately with others and be an intimate spouse. Fearing their own vulnerability, they hide behind a mask of superiority. Marriage then suffers because it is the balance of power, vulnerability, sensitivity, and caring which are essential to an intimate and spiritual relationship. Making the meek blessed would allow a woman to value her compassion and use it to complement her striving for power and autonomy. For men meekness would complement their striving for power with an ability to relate compassionately and vulnerably. In marriage, the traditional roles would be set free, allowing both men and women to become more fully human, more whole and complete.

In pastoral marital therapy, qualities of both partners are nurtured when meekness can be integrated. Fears of accepting the meek parts of the self can result in distorted and inflated self concepts.

"Many that are first shall be last and the last first" (Mt 19:30).

One aspect of the definition of an intimate relationship is the ability of two people at a peer level to be vulnerable and open with one another. One of the blocks to genuine intimacy in a relationship is feelings of superiority and/or inferiority in which the two partners are not peers but rather parent-child or leader-follower. Due to generalized fears of initimacy, frequently based on fears of rejection, spouses often act superior or inferior to protect themselves from having to be intimate or show their more vulnerable sides. For example, if one spouse feels superior in intelligence, ability, or competence, and lets the other know it, then the spouse will most often react with anger and resentment or perhaps feelings of inferiority. Conversely, communication of inferiority by one spouse can, at first hearing, sound vulnerable, but actually be an attempt to elicit sympathy. This can rob the ability of the partner to be direct or confrontative out of the fear of "hurting" the vulnerable partner. In either case intimacy within the marriage will suffer.

Jesus did not intend, when he said that the "first shall be last" (Mt 19:30), that in a marriage there should be no striving for leadership or constructive use of power. A Christian spouse needs the ability to lead and exert influence. The difference is between the striving for greatness, and the believing that one is great. The spouse who is striving for greatness from the perspective of Christian wholeness welcomes the growth and aspirations of the partner. The spouse who believes that he/she is the "greatest," or the "first," based on the feelings of superiority or inferiority described above, will frequently be threatened by the growth and development, personal or professional, of his/her partner. In believing that one is "great," a person is less conscious of the weaker, more dependent parts of the self, and will then block the route to the kingdom of God.

Within a systemic understanding, as with judgment, it is also true that believing oneself to be "first" has some reciprocal consequences. For example, a spouse will say, "My desires come first," and verbally or non-verbally suggest that the partner's desires are secondary. The result is often a rebellious or resistant attitude in the "second" partner which results in a desire to undermine or ignore the "first" spouse. Typical dialogues would be:

Husband — I insist that you clean the house tomorrow!
Wife   — I'll clean when I say I'm ready to clean.

or

Wife   — I want you home at six and absolutely no later!
Husband — Good luck!

Attempting to be "first" often results in the establishment of a parent-child interaction in the marital dyad.

A person who strives for greatness, or to be "first" in relationship to the marital partner, will most likely end up diminished and feeling quite powerless or "last." It is important for the pastoral marital therapist to point out these defensive postures so that a partner who seeks to be "first" will be able to understand the anger and the diminishing behavior of the partner who fears being "last."

"Who is the greatest in the kingdom of heaven? . . . Whosoever humbles himself like this child, he is the greatest in the kingdom of heaven" (Mt 18:1, 4).

Humility is often a difficult and poorly defined concept for married individuals. For some, humility means never asserting oneself, never speaking up, especially when it might cause conflict. For others, humility is seen as a virtue. In either case, false humility is powerful and often used to create distance by engendering guilt and feelings of inferiority in a partner. For example, the husband, who is always "good," a generous giver to the church, and never raises his voice, relates to his more human and emotional wife in a condescending manner. His wife, in part, because of his behavior, feels inferior and creates even more distance. These forms of humility are usually defensive protections from the awareness of negative feelings and fears of rejection. They are a classic example of making a virtue of one's sins.

The humility of which Jesus speaks refers, in a marriage, to the position one partner should have in relationship to the other. The position is neither superior or grandiose, nor inept or unworthy. It should be the position of a humble child, full of awe and wonder leading each person to search for understanding and deeper meaning. It is such a spirit which the pastoral marital therapist will try to create within the therapeutic setting. In so doing the therapist will confront the couple each time one partner attempts to block self-understanding by being superior or inferior. In viewing self-understanding and responsibility as the underlying process of therapeutic growth, the pastoral marital therapist begins to be sensitive to the defenses, hidden attitudes and behaviors that spouses use to block growth.

4. Marital Process Considerations as More Important Than Content

"You will know them by their fruits" (Mt 7:16).

Jesus was sensitive to the superficial ways in which people relate to others. He spoke out against the hypocrite who talks a great deal but says very little. In marriages, as in all human relationships, people are much less affected by what a person says he/she will do than by what is actually done. In families, children rarely listen to what a parent says to do, but react more to what the parent actually does. In marriages, a spouse will learn not to respond nearly so much to what is said, but more to what is acted upon and demonstrated. The words "I love you" are often used destructively in this manner. A husband or wife will say, in a rote manner, "I love you" but will not reinforce it with tonal or behavioral expressions of affection. Another example is when a husband might say to his wife that her professional growth is very important to him, but when she goes to school he refuses to take on more responsibility with the children and is annoyed when she does not have dinner ready on time. His wife will eventually respond negatively to his behavior and ignore his words of support.

In marital therapy, the difference between what is said and what is acted upon is sometimes called the difference between content and process. Content refers to the words, the subject matter being shared by a partner. Process considerations include non-verbal communication, attitude, affect, etc., which are often the context in which the content is communicated. In the examination of marriages, process considerations are equally if not more important than the content of what is said. Process needs to be understood in the same light as the words of Jesus which emphasized matters of the heart, "You shall know them by their fruits" (Mt 7:16).

Beginning pastoral and marital therapists often make the mistake of listening and responding to content rather than process. For this reason alone the true dynamics of the couple can be poorly assessed and treated. For example, a husband states that he wants his wife to complete her education and grow in independence. However, at the same time he is disgusted that the children aren't being cared for "properly." What he says and what he means are two different things. Because the pastor was listening to the first content of what the husband was saying he missed the amount of guilt the husband was actually placing on his wife.

The ability to produce "good fruits" is based on many things. Of utmost importance is the development of a healthy self-concept and identity. As will be discussed, these cannot be developed without a restructuring of the parent-child relationship into an adult-adult relationship.

5. The Necessity of Boundaries for Marital Satisfaction

"For this reason a man/women should leave his/her father and mother and unite with his/her wife/husband" (Good News Bible: Mk 10:7).

The original bonds between a parent and a child are crucial for a child's development. However, if the bonds and the loyalty that a child feels continue into adulthood in a childlike manner, it is very difficult for the child to develop an identity separate from the parents. Similarly, in regard to an individual's relationship to the Lord, if separation between parent and child does not take place, it is difficult for the "child" of any age to approach his/her faith with personal conviction, with attitudes separate from those of his/her parents, or with perspectives based on love rather than fear. Separation and boundaries between a parent and child are for the purpose of enabling a person to approach God with his/her own thought and conviction. The separation begins the process of establishing boundaries enabling the growth and maturation so crucial for a healthy marriage.

When Jesus suggested that in order for a person to cleave to a husband or a wife he/she must leave his/her mother and father, leaving does not mean termination of the relationship, but rather a restructuring. A person will no longer relate to his/her parents from the position of a dependent child. Instead the new relationship will be characterized by adult to adult communication and support. Without such a separation and restructuring of the relationship continual questions of who is to be loyal to whom and who has power over whom will constantly arise between husband, wife, parents, and in-laws. Too often, Jesus' words are not heeded, and an individual's identity is not formed adequately. Thus marriages suffer.

The role of the pastoral marital therapist in this area is to first assess both the current and the historical relationship of each of the marital partners with their own parents, and, second, to enable the couple to see where restructuring of the parent-child relationship was not done and is intruding upon their current marital relationship.

This lack of constructive separation and boundary formation between a parent and child, and consequent lack of identity formation within the individual, is perhaps the most significant factor in marital disharmony. Lack of separation and boundary formation result in a number of marital dynamics. First, a son or daughter will have primary loyalty to one or both parents. This creates competition among all parties, but specifically between one's spouse and parents. If this relationship is poor, lack of separation by the "child" is often the reason. The result for the "child" is the feeling that he/she is being pulled apart in what systems theory calls a "split loyalty." Second, lack of separation makes it difficult for a son or daughter to set boundaries with his/her parents. Boundary, in this case, means to separate from adequately, to be able to express needs and desires with a parent from the position of an adult without fear of being rejected or overwhelmed. A lack of boundaries, due to lack of separation, results in the classical examples of the parents who come to their child's new marriage and home and decide that the furniture is not situated correctly, or the meal is not served in the correct fashion. Third, lack of separation and or boundaries usually results in feelings within the adult "child" of being smothered or overpowered by the parent. Often, this adult "child" will similarly feel smothered and overwhelmed by the spouse. The dynamics which occur in the relationship with either or both parents are often repeated in a parallel fashion between the "child" of these parents and his/her spouse. Fourth, if a person's identity is not adequately formed, the possibility that an individual will be able to maintain adequate separation from one's spouse without exaggerated neediness or fears is slim. Adequate separation means that neither partner will need the other in such a way that one is overly dependent upon the spouse for a positive self-concept or feelings of inclusion or protection.

A key for all of the above is knowledge of and acceptance of as many parts of the self as possible. But how is this done, and what does Jesus offer to facilitate this growth?

6. Reconciliation

"Your sins are forgiven you" (Lk 5:20).

A common theme in all of the scriptural passages mentioned above is the emphasis which Jesus placed on acceptance of all parts of the self. He realized that meekness, fear, ineptitude, ignorance, vulnerability, etc., were aspects of the self that many people were and are afraid to address and integrate into the self. "Since the evil facts are as genuine parts of nature as the good ones, the philosophic assumption should be that they have some rational significance, and that systematic healthy mindedness, failing as it does to accord to sorrow, pain, and death, any positive or active attention, is formally less complete than systems that at least try to include these elements in their scope, such as Christianity" (James, 1961, p. 141). Instead of accepting these "evil facts" people often repress and deny them and then project them onto other family members. Some children and partners do not have the strength or the knowledge to refuse these "gifts" and begin to view themselves in a distorted fashion. In the most constructive form of self-love a person is not afraid to look at both the positive and the negative aspects of the self. Consequently, spouses and children do not have to be recipients of negative projections. There is an attempt by each individual to love all aspects of the self and demonstrate "good fruits."

How does a person accept all these difficult parts of the self when so much of social learning teaches people to hide from fears and hurts and the negative aspects of what it means to live and grow? Jesus gave people not only the intellectual understanding but also the means to integrate that which we so often want to give away. First, Jesus preached the forgiveness of sins. If the concept of transcendent forgiveness is truly integrated and applied an individual would not have to hide from the parts of the self which are difficult to accept. Second, God's acceptance of humanity, symbolized by the gift of his Son in human flesh, if believed, can give an individual the power to accept all of his/her own humanity. Christ's forgiveness and acceptance can give an individual the courage and opportunity to look at personal successes and failures, strengths and weaknesses, and have them all become a part of the fabric of life. Without this perspective they can easily be seen as abhorrent and projected onto another person. Such forgiveness, when applied, and acceptance, when integrated and felt, is the process of reconciliation. While no one attains it, the closer one comes to reconciling all parts of the self the healthier one becomes.

A marriage made up of two partners who accept Christ's forgiveness will be characterized by the struggle to understand one another and look at their own complicity for the failures or difficulties in the relationship. A Christian marriage is made up of two individuals who are not afraid to ask, "What am I contributing to the problem?" and "How am I enhancing my own growth and that of my partner?" The goal for the Christian, in enhancing the sanctity of marriage, is to use Christ's gifts of forgiveness of sins and acceptance of humanity to become more psychologically honest. This psychological honesty is more a journey than a destination: it is the journey of self-reflection and movement toward knowledge of all parts of the self; it is taking the divided self and uniting it through the power of the Holy Spirit. "This innate striving for wholeness is the decisive factor in any real understanding of the process whereby healing is brought about by consciousness" (Phillips, 1948, p. 31).

The role of the pastoral marital therapist is to limit judgments, teach self-responsibility, and provide a context in which both individuals and the couple will seek continual understanding and spiritual wholeness on route toward the kingdom of God.

Conclusion

The pastoral marital therapist, in order to be true to each word of the title, needs to integrate and implement a theological and a psychological perspective in the practice of marital therapy. The uniqueness of pastoral marital therapy is evident in such integration.

The Holy Spirit, often blocked by conflict and pain in an individual or couple, is the energy for pastoral therapy. If guided by the Holy Spirit, the direction taken by the individual will be toward reconciling all aspects of the self. Ending the judgments and blaming between partners is the foremost role of the pastoral therapist. In judgment the darker sides of the soul are projected onto a spouse instead of understood by the individual. Furthermore judgment is reciprocal in that judgments given are usually received.

Often blocking the Holy Spirit and processes of reconciliation are feelings of superiority and inferiority communicated by marital couples. The ability to create and maintain a peer relationship in which the needs of both self and partner are considered is crucial for the development of intimacy and self-understanding.

The intent and actions which characterize a couple's communication are equally if not more important than the content. The ability to assess the process issues of a couple and not get inducted into the content is often a weak area for beginning pastoral marital therapists and requires continual supervision.

Finally, Jesus was interested in boundaries and separation as crucial for individual growth and the development of faith. A boundary between God and people is as important as a boundary for the individual and the marital dyad. Without boundaries there is little development of personal identity or marital harmony.

As a framework for all of the above, it is the reconciling power of Jesus Christ enacted and integrated into the individual and marital dyad which is the goal of the pastoral marital therapist.

References

James, W. *The Varieties of Religious Experience*. New York: Collier, 1961.

Niebuhr, R. *The Nature and Destiny of Man.* New York: Scribner's, 1941.

Phillips, D., Howes, E., and Nixon, L. (eds.). *The Choice Is Always Ours.* New York: Harper and Row, 1948.

Sanford, J. *Jesus, Paul and Depth Psychology.* Pa: Religious Publishing, 1948.

For Further Reading

Niebuhr, R. *The Nature and Destiny of Man.* New York: Collier, 1961.

Phillips, D., Howes, E., and Nixon, L. (eds.). *The Choice Is Always Ours.* New York: Harper and Row, 1948. **A study in differentiation.**

Sanford, John A. *The Man Who Wrestled with God.* New Jersey: Paulist Press, 1981. **A study of differentiation and individuation.**

Singer, June. *Boundaries of the Soul.* New York: Anchor Press, 1973. **Jungian psychology.**

clude courses in general systems theory, marital
therapy, and individual psychopathology with
e. A basic understanding of systemic behavior,
tergenerational loyalties, defense mechanisms,
how all of these are related to assessment,
, and intervention techniques is crucial. With-
nding, the pastor should limit his/her involve-
referral work, which is discussed later in this
, the pastor receives such an education (and
be advisable) he/she needs to be involved in
n of the therapeutic work. This supervision, if
ken from an Approved Supervisor of the Amer-
Marriage and Family Therapy. A second, and
hoice, would be supervision from a Fellow or
erican Association of Pastoral Counselors or a
sychologist if, and only if, such a person has a
perience in working with systems theory and
not solely individually oriented in his/her ap-
ly, or almost exclusively, individualistic ap-
ul to marriages and families due to its lack of
interrelatedness and interdependence of be-
ists frequently separate marital partners for
course.) In addition, such an approach is more
oral counseling center, for reasons mentioned
transference and repressed feelings which are
nto the pastoral therapist. Professional super-
doing therapy within his/her congregation
is is both for the continual edification of the
protection. A supervisor can point out lack of
and aspects of transference and countertrans-
nost experienced therapists can be blind to.
and continuing supervision, a network of
essionals is very advantageous. An opportu-
ons with other marital therapists and a per-
a psychiatrist for client medications or
it. Many pastoral marital therapists who end
narriage, or destroying their own careers, are
ecurity and/or arrogant state, say, "I know it

Chapter 2

Pastoral Marital Therapy Within the Local Church

Within the local church, pastoral marital therapy affords many opportunities for enriching marriage and family life and broadening the
ministries of clergy and lay leaders. There are two basic church related contexts in which pastoral marital therapy is done. The first is
the pastoral counseling center. Such a center is most often staffed by
full time professional pastoral counselors who do not, as a general
rule, lead worship, do visitation, or get involved in the general pastoral ministry of the church. Such a center may use church facilities
and frequently identifies its staff as being separate from the everyday
functioning of the church. Other centers have totally separate physical facilities and staff. The second context occurs when the pastor or
lay leader engages in the practice of pastoral marital therapy, as well
as being involved in the general ministry of the church.

What makes these contexts so different is that in the pastoral
counseling center therapists wear only "one hat" and are not otherwise directly involved in a leadership capacity with their clients in
worship on Sunday mornings or at weddings, funerals, etc. The pastor or lay worker who includes the practice of marital therapy within
his/her job description wears "many hats" and may thus be involved
with clients in many different religious, educational and social settings. The first context has more clearly established pastoral and
therapeutic boundaries; the wearing of "one hat" allows for a very
defined therapist role, which protects and defines the therapist-
client relationship. In the second context, the wearing of "many
hats" often results in diffuse boundaries and lack of role definition.
In that context, instead of the boundaries being established a priori
by the structure of the setting, there is a need for the pastoral marital
therapist to establish and define them. (In actuality, both pastoral
therapist and client couple need to take responsibility for establish-

27

ing appropriate boundaries.) It is this second context which will be the main focus of this chapter. While the points being made will also be applicable, at differing levels, to the worker in a pastoral counseling center, the pastor or lay worker doing marital therapy within the general context of a local church is in a far more complex situation which necessitates continual heightened attention and regard.

Proponents of individual psychotherapy, spiritually oriented or not, relying so much on theories of regression and transference, have long stated that therapy should not be done by the clergy of the client's congregation. In individual psychotherapy, especially that which is conducted from an Ego Psychology perspective, regressive behavior and repressed feelings are often elicited. Such feelings might be exaggerated emotions of love, hate, anger, or abandonment, all of which, if not well boundaried, and limited to the therapeutic session, could be potentially very problematic for the parishioner and/or the pastor as well as the general welfare of the church. For example, a pastor felt himself to be knowledgeable in the practice of individual psychotherapy and invited a depressed woman parishioner into therapy. This woman had been abandoned by her father as a child. The woman transferred feelings toward her father, that of wanting desperately to be loved, and feelings of rage that she wasn't, onto the pastor. In a pastoral counseling center, with a therapist whose sole job it was to be a therapist for this woman, such a transference would most likely be helpful to both elicit repressed feeling and allow for healing and reparenting within the therapist-client relationship. However, the therapy in this example was not done in a pastoral counseling center. The pastor talked with her at his own home, most often for longer than a therapeutic hour. During the same period both pastor and client were involved in sharing weekend long church retreats and Sunday morning worship. In part, the needs of the woman, matched with the desire and need of the pastor to be "helpful," along with the lengthy amount of time they spent together in various situations, resulted in the woman having greatly exaggerated feelings toward her pastor. When she voiced these feelings of love and affection, the pastor, due to his inexperience, remarked that he was very faithful to his wife. His client felt this to be another abandonment, however, and this time vented her rage by telling a few "key" people in the church that the pastor had

made advances to
though the "facts"
pastor's career w
narios do end up i
ful family and ch

The easiest
with parishioners
a good idea, it i
leader of a Chris
Counselor, to th
come to the past
sel. A premise c
therapy in many
people will com
lay leaders. Fur
of the psychiatri
them, less of a s
miliar with thei
only the psycho
ical concerns su
addition, in ma
vicinity with a
emotional desp

Therefore
be done by the
equate guideli
pastoral marita
Such guidelin
such as: (1) ed
personal boun
(5) client boun
the church; (7

1. Education

A pastor
marital thera
and continui

minimum, should in
and family theory an
a systems perspectiv
behavioral change, ir
psychodynamics, an
therapeutic planning
out such an understa
ment in therapy to
primer. As, and afte
more courses would
continuing supervisic
possible, should be ta
ican Association for N
often equally strong c
Diplomate in the Am
local psychiatrist or p
sound training and e
marital therapy and is
proach. An exclusive
proach is often harmf
consideration for the
haviors. (Such therap
therapy, as a matter of
applicable for the past
previously concerning
frequently projected o
vision for the pastor
should never stop. Th
pastor, and for his/her
boundaries, induction,
ference that even the

Besides education
peers and helping pro
nity for case presentat
sonal relationship wit
consultation is importa
up harming a client, a r
people who, in their in

all and don't need consultations or feedback." Such pastors can play out a role of an isolated and insecure religious worker who "alone" can bring comfort to God's people. Real strength and competence can perhaps be better measured by one's ability to accept limitations, request, listen to and integrate constructive feedback.

With an appropriate and continuing education and competent ongoing supervision, the next important variable to consider is the setting within the church in which marital therapy is going to be practiced.

2. *Appropriate Settings*

A private setting and general privacy are key for doing pastoral marital therapy within the church. One aspect of privacy is that the office for doing therapy should be as soundproof as possible and the office entrance as private as can be reasonably arranged. It is helpful if there is a waiting room which is not in the church secretary's office or any other such public place. General discretion is very important. A client should never be seen for therapy in the pastor's home, unless there is a private and separate office with an outside entrance. Therapy is a professional relationship, and a formal setting adds to the seriousness of everyone concerned. In addition, clients should not be seen late at night when the church is empty, but, whenever possible, during the day or early evening at typical office hours.

In the office, the telephone should not need to be answered nor should someone be able to knock on the door. Remedies for the above include a secretary who can screen calls, an answering machine, keeping the phone off the hook during the session, and notifying the congregation that the phone will not be answered at certain times. A simple sign stating "Do not disturb" will most often be sufficient to prevent disturbance.

The office should be arranged so that clients and pastoral therapist sit in chairs of equal height, not on a couch, and without a desk in between. A therapist sitting in a chair which is higher or lower than the clients can create difficulties in joining and relating. The scenario of the couple sitting on a couch looking at the pastor often tends to make the pastor the center of attention, instead of the most often preferred role of the facilitator for the couple's communication. Lighting should not be seductively dim, yet not so bright as to convey the impression of being in an examining room.

The office environment is very important and needs to ensure privacy and confidentiality. Intrusion by answering the phone or a knock on the door, uncomfortable furniture or inappropriate lighting can be disruptive to the entire session. Attention to these matters can be a sign to the couple that the pastoral therapist is a professional who is there for them and not preoccupied with other matters.

3. *Personal Boundaries for the Pastoral Marital Therapist*

In addition to education, continual supervision, and counseling setting there are other important considerations which determine whether therapy done in the church is appropriate or not. One of the most important of these considerations is the issue of the personal boundaries of the pastoral marital therapist.

The concept of a personal boundary is a construct which helps to define and judge whether the verbal and non-verbal/behavioral messages and statements of the pastoral therapist are discrete, thoughtful, and appropriate in consideration of the role(s) of pastor/ therapist and parishioner(s)/client(s). Awareness of and emphasis on the respect and integrity of the clients in the differing social situations of the church is one indication of appropriate boundaries. A lack of boundaries results in a disregard for confidentiality and an inability to appropriately choose what emotions and information should be communicated, and to whom, at any given time. A demonstration of personal boundaries by the pastor will give the couple faith that what they might share in confidence to the pastor will be held in confidence and treated with respect. What is meant by respect is that even if the pastor disagrees with the ethical or moral situation of the clients, he/she will continue to be a representative of reconciliation and work toward client understanding and healing—and, if that is not possible, to make an appropriate referral. The couple needs to trust that whatever they say will not be taken personally, overreacted to, or repeated to anyone in the church. Furthermore, the couples of the congregation who want to come for therapy in the church need some confidence that the pastor will not ask them about appointment times or engage in discussion about therapy after the church service, or in any other social setting. Further boundaries which are needed are demonstrated by the pastor's ability to relate naturally and normally outside the therapeutic setting, as he/she relates to other couples in the various church functions. By "natural," what is meant is that the pastor won't draw attention to the relationship as different from his/her relationship to other couples in the church. This is difficult for the pastor whose own emotions are not bounded sufficiently.

What is also needed to bound the therapy from the rest of the church context is a discussion with clients on the preaching and the teaching done by the pastor for the entire church. It will often seem to the clients, and perhaps sometimes rightly so, that the pastoral therapist will be discussing, in his/her sermon, what the couple talked about in their previous counseling session. This clearly can create all sorts of misunderstanding and emotional trauma. It is suggested that the therapist explain this dynamic to the couple at the outset of any therapeutic relationship and urge the couple to speak to him/her if they feel that their issues were aired in public. The pastor must be sure not to use specific client couples to illustrate, even anonymously, material for homilies or sermons.

Two other areas of importance are the type of clothing worn and the general affect of the pastoral marital therapist. Client couples who are coming for help are often quite without boundaries. This means, for instance, that they might be feeling smothered or invaded by their partner, or they might be judging and blaming the other. If the therapist is also seen as without boundaries, further chaos and mistrust can develop. What the author would call inappropriate clothing (for the Northeast U.S. and could vary for other parts of the country) might be the male pastor wearing no coat or tie, a shirt unbuttoned to show a gold chain, with dungarees and sneakers. While the clothes certainly do not make the therapist they certainly are often a silent testimonial to the level of maturity, separateness and competence of the pastor. At the other end of the continuum would be the pastor who publicly rarely wears clerical garb, but does so for the counseling sessions, creating too rigid a boundary. The point is to be appropriate and aware of the effect of one's dress upon the counseling relationship.

Appropriate and bounded affect is a difficult dynamic to describe. By affect, what is meant is the amount of emotion which the pastor uses when he/she relates to his/her clients. Preaching or teaching, for instance, with a loud aggressive voice will often be experienced as invasive by the clients. If the pastor's affect is seductive, conciliatory, or condescending, other destructive dynamics ensue. What is needed, and often developed with the help of a supervisor, is a bounded affect, in which a variety of emotions and thoughts can be shared in a context of respect for the clients' integrity. Such sharing of emotion or thought will be for the benefit of the couple and not self-serving for the pastor, or the consequence of the pastor's lack of control. Inappropriate affect by the pastor is most often a symptom of his/her own lack of growth in the particular area being discussed. For instance, the pastor who cannot deal with a client's anger most likely has unresolved feelings about anger in his/her own background. Insight into one's affect is best received through feedback from a supervisor or other marital therapists.

One more boundary, which is perhaps the most important, is demonstrated in the pastor's firm grasp of his/her own limitations. It is a sign of competence to be able to recognize what issues are beyond one's skill level and when referral is the most appropriate counsel. Unfortunately, many pastors overestimate their counseling skills and abilities, and become "rescuers." They can become blind to their personal and professional limits to appropriately affect change and bring about healing, actually causing harm to persons and relationships.

4. Contract Therapy

Besides the importance of the pastoral marital therapist having appropriate boundaries the therapy in and of itself needs to have limits and definitions. Working with church couples in marital therapy should not be open-ended. Open-ended therapy means that there is no framework of time, either for the length of the counseling session or for the duration of therapy.

Contracting means that the couple and the pastor agree to meet for a sixty minute session and probably no longer. An hour is a sufficient length of time to address the important issues of the couple.

It is not so long that the session will be unfocused or cover far too many topics for any individual or couple to be able to absorb. If a couple knows that the pastor will not limit the length of time spent in a session they might not come in the first place. Another possibility would be to spend the first hour filling the session with chatter, and avoiding the important feelings and issues which need to be discussed. The limiting of the time is a key to focusing the session on relevant material, intensifying the work and the power of the session, "winding down," and setting an appropriate boundary between the couple and the pastoral marital therapist. In contrast, a friend would probably not place a time limit on most discussions nor would he/she set parameters on what was appropriate to discuss and what was not. Therapy is not getting together in an unstructured way to chat, but a focused and structured time and format for insight and healing.

The overall length of marital therapy done in the church setting also needs to be placed into some framework of time. Many experienced pastoral marital therapists will state something like, "Let's meet together for three sessions (maximum of six) so that we can get to know one another better and explore whether pastoral marital therapy will be productive and meaningful for you. At the end of those sessions, let's talk about whether to continue, stop, or whether I should refer you." (See references on assessment in Chapter 4.) Such contracting by the therapist and the couple allows for several positive dynamics: (1) client couples, whose schedules are often difficult to coordinate, will be less reluctant to enter therapy because there are some limits placed on its duration, and it is not an open ended process; (2) the pastoral therapist will realistically give himself/herself time to assess the needs of the couple and determine whether his/her skills match those particular needs; (3) because the couple realizes the limitation placed on time, they are more likely to use the therapy time they have more productively; (4) if referral proves to be the best option, the couple will not feel as abandoned by the pastor because the possibility of referral was brought up in the first session.

If the pastoral therapist and the couple chose to establish a longer-term therapeutic relationship, certain limitations should be imposed. While there are no hard and fast rules, six to twenty sessions would be considered longer-term work. Over twenty sessions in a church context needs to be considered very carefully with concern about the maintenance of therapeutic boundaries, dependence of the couple, and protection of the pastoral therapist's time. Seeing couples for over one half a year (twenty-six sessions) should be limited in the number of couples seen and reserved for couples who are both growing over time and fit the outline for client boundaries described below.

5. *Client Boundaries*

It would be a mistake to suggest that because the setting is correct and the pastor is appropriately trained and competent, and because clear contracting guidelines exist, pastoral marital therapy can then begin without consideration of whether the client-couple fulfills certain guidelines for being seen within the church context.

Not only do the therapeutic setting and the pastoral therapist need strong definition and boundaries; so do the client-couples who will be seen within the framework of the church's ministry. There are no hard and fast rules for what type of client to see in the church, but there are some important considerations. For instance, is one or both of the spouses a member of the Board of Deacons or the Parish Council? Is the client couple the pastor's next door neighbor? The same people who are responsible for the pastor's salary or who are supervising the therapist lay workers with church education probably should not be seen in the church by the therapist/pastor or therapist/layworker. It is very common for a couple with the therapist to experience many diverse feelings such as fear, anger, distance, etc. Despite the best of intentions, it would be difficult if these feelings did not stay within the context of therapy and instead became a topic of, for example, the next deacons' meeting.

The client-couples also need to be instructed in the importance of confidentiality. One suggestion for the pastoral marital therapist is to tell the couple something like, "I certainly won't discuss what we talk about and I expect you to similarly honor the confidentiality." Client couples in the church need to be coached to refrain from saying, "Our pastor said . . . " This statement will be inevitably misquoted and misinterpreted by either the couple or the interested church member they are relating to.

If the clients cannot keep the therapy from being a discussion during coffee hour, at board meetings, or with friends, they should not be seen by the pastor within the context of their own church and should be referred.

6. *Appropriate Therapeutic Schools for the Church Setting*

There are different ways of understanding and conducting marital therapy. Each theory has a different set of principles and assumptions, only some of which are appropriate for a pastoral marital therapist to use within the church setting.

As alluded to previously, long-term individual psychotherapy, with its emphasis on regression and transference, would probably not be appropriate for the pastor and a parishioner. There would be too much opportunity for the defined boundaries of therapy to spill over into the life and the work of the church.

Pastoral marital counseling does not rely as heavily on regression and transference, especially in reference to the relationship of either spouse and the pastoral therapist. Instead, in marital therapy conducted within the church, behavioral, structural, communication, social learning and family of origin theories are stressed. These theories work with more present-oriented behaviors, skills, insights, and emotions without the need for regression or transference, and are thus well suited for therapy by the pastor within his/her congregation. What regression there is, in marital therapy, is most often seen in the intimate relationships and projections between the two spouses, not between one spouse, or both, and the pastoral therapist. Because of this, the intensity of feeling when working on early experiences of abandonment or rejection, for instance, is less likely to be placed on the pastoral therapist. The chances, therefore, that these feelings become acted out within the church are diminished but certainly not removed entirely.

The sharing of the feelings which get projected onto each spouse by the other can potentially be managed by the therapist without being placed in the position of being the object of the emotional intensity. This is most frequently accomplished by making certain that said feelings are consistently related to current behavior and relationships instead of being the sought after goal in and of themselves.

7. Education and Fees

A final step in establishing a practice of pastoral marital therapy
is the education of the church as to the nature of such therapy, how
it fits into church ministry, and the general importance of boundaries, including the setting of fees.

Successful pastoral marital therapists have done a great deal to
educate their entire church as to what therapy is, and how it is a part
of ministry. Confidentiality is taught as an important dynamic for
families and churches as well as specifically for marriages and marital
therapy. Non-judgmental and self-responsible ways of relating need
to be preached, taught and exemplified by the pastor. Through all
the vehicles of education within the church the pastor communicates
that it is the church and the reconciliation of Jesus Christ to which
troubled couples and individuals who are in pain can turn. Further
education is needed as to the uniqueness of the pastoral marital
counselor's role. The pastor involved in marital therapy uses tools
which the secular therapist frequently does not have or use, those
being the Bible, prayer, and a context of faith. These tools, when
appropriately and sensitively used, can provide great comfort and
healing and deepen the integration of the therapy or counseling experience.

One area for needed education of the church members, and specifically for the trustees (or equivalent), would be the charging of
fees. The amount of the fee is secondary to the charging of the fee in
the first place. A fee sets a boundary between the pastor and the couple which helps reinforce that therapy is not a meeting of friends or
an informal gathering. Without boundaries, such as fees, it is easier
for the pastor to be inducted into the destructive rules of the marital
system, thus losing some objectivity and often being rendered ineffective to alter dysfunctional marital patterns. In addition, the fee
reduces the amount of indebtedness the client couple will feel
toward the therapist. Such indebtedness can be destructively used
by the pastor to talk a couple into continuing therapy past the point
of helpfulness. The couple might believe, "The pastor has given
us so much; how can we leave him/her now?" Without such indebtedness, there is more freedom by clients to both enter and leave
therapy.

Many churches refuse the pastor permission to charge fees on the grounds that providing pastoral marital therapy is part of the minister's existing responsibilities. Perhaps short term referral counseling is part of the minister's existing role but therapy needs to be viewed in a different way. Fees enhance the movement of the couple, bind the therapist-client relationship, and place the therapy on a different plane than that of a meeting of friends. What is often suggested is that the pastoral therapist's fees, from two dollars on up, depending on ability to pay and the level of competence of the pastor, be placed in a pastor's education fund and be used by the pastoral therapist to pay for his/her continuing supervision and education.

Conclusion

Pastoral marital therapy within the context of the church is an enrichment of the church's responsibility and ministry for the care of souls. This ministry, however, must be done thoughtfully and within certain defined boundaries. The pastor or lay worker engaged in such a ministry needs a sound education in systems theory and marital therapy, along with current and ongoing supervision. There must be an appropriate setting which provides privacy and confidentiality. The pastor must be boundaried in all behavior, respecting his/her client's integrity, maintaining confidentiality, and knowing the limits of his/her skills. The therapy itself needs to be formally structured in a therapeutic hour, and a contract clearly established at the beginning, of from three to six weeks, to determine whether the process is healthy and constructive for everyone. The clients also must agree to honor certain rules of privacy and confidentiality, especially with church members and neighbors. Certain modes of doing therapy are more appropriate than others in the context of the church, and such modes need to provide the grounding for pastoral marital therapy. Finally the church needs to be educated as to what pastoral marital therapy is, and how it is best structured within the church setting. Fees are one aspect of this definition and serve to enhance therapy and allow for the pastoral therapist to create a fund for continuing supervision and education.

For Further Reading

Anderson, D. *New Approaches to Family Pastoral Care.* Philadelphia: Fortress Press, 1980.

Clinebell, H. *Growth Counseling for Marriage Enrichment.* Philadelphia: Fortress Press, 1975.

Wynn, J.S. *Family Therapy in Pastoral Ministry.* San Francisco: Harper & Row, 1982. **Integration of systems approaches with applications to ministry**

Chapter 2

Pastoral Marital Therapy Within the Local Church

Within the local church, pastoral marital therapy affords many opportunities for enriching marriage and family life and broadening the ministries of clergy and lay leaders. There are two basic church related contexts in which pastoral marital therapy is done. The first is the pastoral counseling center. Such a center is most often staffed by full time professional pastoral counselors who do not, as a general rule, lead worship, do visitation, or get involved in the general pastoral ministry of the church. Such a center may use church facilities and frequently identifies its staff as being separate from the everyday functioning of the church. Other centers have totally separate physical facilities and staff. The second context occurs when the pastor or lay leader engages in the practice of pastoral marital therapy, as well as being involved in the general ministry of the church.

What makes these contexts so different is that in the pastoral counseling center therapists wear only "one hat" and are not otherwise directly involved in a leadership capacity with their clients in worship on Sunday mornings or at weddings, funerals, etc. The pastor or lay worker who includes the practice of marital therapy within his/her job description wears "many hats" and may thus be involved with clients in many different religious, educational and social settings. The first context has more clearly established pastoral and therapeutic boundaries; the wearing of "one hat" allows for a very defined therapist role, which protects and defines the therapist-client relationship. In the second context, the wearing of "many hats" often results in diffuse boundaries and lack of role definition. In that context, instead of the boundaries being established a priori by the structure of the setting, there is a need for the pastoral marital therapist to establish and define them. (In actuality, both pastoral therapist and client couple need to take responsibility for establish-

ing appropriate boundaries.) It is this second context which will be
the main focus of this chapter. While the points being made will also
be applicable, at differing levels, to the worker in a pastoral counseling center, the pastor or lay worker doing marital therapy within
the general context of a local church is in a far more complex situation
which necessitates continual heightened attention and regard.

Proponents of individual psychotherapy, spiritually oriented or
not, relying so much on theories of regression and transference, have
long stated that therapy should not be done by the clergy of the
client's congregation. In individual psychotherapy, especially that
which is conducted from an Ego Psychology perspective, regressive
behavior and repressed feelings are often elicited. Such feelings
might be exaggerated emotions of love, hate, anger, or abandonment, all of which, if not well boundaried, and limited to the therapeutic session, could be potentially very problematic for the
parishioner and/or the pastor as well as the general welfare of the
church. For example, a pastor felt himself to be knowledgeable in
the practice of individual psychotherapy and invited a depressed
woman parishioner into therapy. This woman had been abandoned
by her father as a child. The woman transferred feelings toward her
father, that of wanting desperately to be loved, and feelings of rage
that she wasn't, onto the pastor. In a pastoral counseling center, with
a therapist whose sole job it was to be a therapist for this woman,
such a transference would most likely be helpful to both elicit repressed feeling and allow for healing and reparenting within the
therapist-client relationship. However, the therapy in this example
was not done in a pastoral counseling center. The pastor talked with
her at his own home, most often for longer than a therapeutic hour.
During the same period both pastor and client were involved in sharing weekend long church retreats and Sunday morning worship. In
part, the needs of the woman, matched with the desire and need of
the pastor to be "helpful," along with the lengthy amount of time
they spent together in various situations, resulted in the woman having greatly exaggerated feelings toward her pastor. When she voiced
these feelings of love and affection, the pastor, due to his inexperience, remarked that he was very faithful to his wife. His client felt
this to be another abandonment, however, and this time vented her
rage by telling a few "key" people in the church that the pastor had

made advances toward her and was seeing her in his house. Even though the "facts" as reported by the parishioner were not true, the pastor's career was potentially ruined. Each year many such scenarios do end up in extra-marital affairs and very destructive and sinful family and church relationships.

The easiest solution to the difficulties raised by doing therapy with parishioners is to simply say, "Don't do it!" Yet, even if this was a good idea, it is an unreasonable expectation. From the earliest leader of a Christian group who experienced the Holy Spirit as the Counselor, to the most recent-day pastoral counselor, people have come to the pastor for spiritual and psychological guidance and counsel. A premise of this primer is that no matter what the warnings, therapy in many forms will be done in the church, and that many people will come first, when hurting and in pain, to their pastor or lay leaders. Furthermore, many people will go to the pastor instead of the psychiatrist, psychologist or marital therapist because it is, for them, less of a stigma. They may also have more trust in and are familiar with their pastor, and believe they will be able to address not only the psychological and interpersonal issues but related theological concerns such as hope, despair, the cross, and reconciliation. In addition, in many rural areas, the pastor is the only person in the vicinity with any kind of counseling training to turn to in times of emotional despair.

Therefore, instead of fruitlessly saying that therapy should not be done by the clergy for their congregants, what is needed are adequate guidelines for who should participate, when and how, when pastoral marital therapy is done within the framework of the church. Such guidelines must be established after consideration of issues such as: (1) education and supervision; (2) appropriate settings; (3) personal boundaries for the pastoral therapist; (4) contract therapy; (5) client boundaries; (6) appropriate therapeutic schools for use in the church; (7) church education and fees.

1. Education and Supervision

A pastor or lay worker who is going to be involved in pastoral marital therapy needs to have both a sound theoretical background, and continuing supervision of his/her work. Education, at the very minimum, should include courses in general systems theory, marital and family theory and therapy, and individual psychopathology with a systems perspective. A basic understanding of systemic behavior, behavioral change, intergenerational loyalties, defense mechanisms, psychodynamics, and how all of these are related to assessment, therapeutic planning, and intervention techniques is crucial. Without such an understanding, the pastor should limit his/her involvement in therapy to referral work, which is discussed later in this primer. As, and after, the pastor receives such an education (and more courses would be advisable) he/she needs to be involved in continuing supervision of the therapeutic work. This supervision, if possible, should be taken from an Approved Supervisor of the American Association for Marriage and Family Therapy. A second, and often equally strong choice, would be supervision from a Fellow or Diplomate in the American Association of Pastoral Counselors or a local psychiatrist or psychologist if, and only if, such a person has a sound training and experience in working with systems theory and marital therapy and is not solely individually oriented in his/her approach. An exclusively, or almost exclusively, individualistic approach is often harmful to marriages and families due to its lack of consideration for the interrelatedness and interdependence of behaviors. (Such therapists frequently separate marital partners for therapy, as a matter of course.) In addition, such an approach is more applicable for the pastoral counseling center, for reasons mentioned previously concerning transference and repressed feelings which are frequently projected onto the pastoral therapist. Professional supervision for the pastor doing therapy within his/her congregation should never stop. This is both for the continual edification of the pastor, and for his/her protection. A supervisor can point out lack of boundaries, induction, and aspects of transference and countertransference that even the most experienced therapists can be blind to.

Besides education and continuing supervision, a network of peers and helping professionals is very advantageous. An opportunity for case presentations with other marital therapists and a personal relationship with a psychiatrist for client medications or consultation is important. Many pastoral marital therapists who end up harming a client, a marriage, or destroying their own careers, are people who, in their insecurity and/or arrogant state, say, "I know it

Chapter 3

Key Concepts in Short Term Marital Counseling

In order to do effective marital counseling, the pastoral therapist must have a solid conceptual background. Different approaches to therapy and the various dynamics inherent and possible within the marital therapy relationship need to be clearly understood. The topics discussed in this chapter are by no means exhaustive. We have selected those concepts which we believe to be most salient for inclusion in a primer of pastoral marital therapy.

Essential Concepts

Beneath the specific concepts presented in this primer there lies a general philosophy that explores the possibilities for growth and change, the reality of individual and relational strengths, the need for appropriate differentiation and reconciliation, and the need to dispel crippling marital myths.

A. *Growth and Change*

Growth and change are essential concepts for all theories of marital therapy, and inherent in the Christian gospel. "The growth model theory implies that each individual, in order to function relatively symptom free, must feel that he/she is growing, producing, and creating in ways that are fitting to him/her" (Luthman, 1974, p. 3). Marriage can be a context for continual growth and development but it can also be a relationship in which stagnation and rigidity are paramount. Most couples who come for therapy have experienced some blocks to personal and relational growth and integration and have come to therapy to understand and alleviate the problems. Many individual attempts to grow within the marriage, such as get-

41

ting angry to alleviate feelings of rejection, are often counter-pro-
ductive. Even so, such attempts to alleviate pain and bring about
movement should be treated with respect and caring by the therapist. "In every piece of behavior, no matter how destructive that behavior appears, there is some level of an intent to grow" (Luthman,
1974, p. 5). Behind a couple's judgments there are frequently fears
of being hurt; behind violence are feelings of powerlessness or perhaps humiliation. Whether the attempts to grow by the couple are
deemed constructive or not, they are worthy of the respect of the
therapist. The pastoral marital therapist believes in the God-given
"natural force" in each person pushing them to grow and develop
through the continual unfolding of the Holy Spirit. While ignorance
and fear might block personal and relational growth and development, the Holy Spirit is continually working to circumvent resistance and lead people into truth and understanding.

B. Strengths

There is a strong tendency in marital therapy to exclusively assess and treat dysfunction. In the initial sessions, information is gathered by the therapist who often continually points to and seeks
elaboration of the difficulties of the couple. While understanding the
negative dynamics is an important aspect of therapy, a pastoral marital therapist needs to diligently seek out individual and couple
strengths as well. This is not particularly difficult to do if the therapist
integrates a pastoral perspective.

The fact that a couple has come for assistance is a strength, a
plus. Instead of being satisfied with hurt and frustration they have a
level of commitment, health and ability to give reconciliation
through counseling a chance. Individuals and couples coming to
therapy have some desire, consciously or unconsciously, to grow and
examine their own complicity in the marital difficulty and thus are
due significant respect and admiration a priori. The positive intention needs to be affirmed.

Every individual has some strengths. The strength might be the
ability to endure and cope with a difficult relationship. There is significant strength shown even by the angry or manipulative spouse in
that these destructive behaviors are usually attempts to protect the

self from hurt and rejection. The pastoral marital therapist must facilitate recognition of each individual's and couple's strengths. If the therapist cannot perceive the strengths, and is oriented only toward the "sinful nature" of the negative interactions, he/she should not work with the clients. Furthermore, if the therapist views one partner as having strengths and the other not, he/she has lost systemic understanding and ought to refer, or at least seek supervision/consultation for the case.

C. Differentiation

The concept of differentiation is a key foundation stone of marital systems theory. A general assumption is that the best marriages are ones in which both partners enter the relationship differentiated from their parents and are able, within the marriage, to continue to be differentiated from each other. Differentiation is the ability of an individual to develop one's own identity and personality apart from parents in particular, and any outside influence in general. A differentiated person will be able to form his/her own thoughts, think through issues independently, and make decisions based on an internal authority without being unduly swayed by other individuals or groups. A differentiated individual will have a balance of emotion and intellect and will be able to appropriately relate out of both spheres. A differentiated marital partner will not continually react to his/her spouse but will be able to be objective, separate, and understanding of his/her own responsibility in a marital difficulty.

Another general assumption in marital theory is that the degree to which an individual is differentiated from his/her parents is about the same degree he/she will be able to be differentiated from his/her spouse. For example, if a man has difficulty talking directly, as an adult, to his mother, similar difficulties will probably appear in relationship to his wife. For this reason many pastoral marital therapists will work with families of origin as well as with the couple.

D. Reconciliation

A major goal of pastoral marital therapy is to bring about reconciliation for the individual and the couple. However, helping the couple to reconcile difficulties and disagreements is only one level of the work which needs to be accomplished. At a more primary level the pastoral marital therapist needs to exemplify and communicate the intentions of Christ as he sought reconciliation for each individual, married or not. By asking each individual to recognize and pull back projections and anger, judgment and blame, Christ asked every individual to find true integration in relationship to self and others. As opposed to other relationships, in the intimacy and intensities of marriages and marital dynamics, there is more of a tendency to project onto a partner unwanted and unconscious parts of the self, and to generally protect the self from rejection and hurt. Therefore, marriages are a unique arena to understand the deeper meanings of reconciliation with oneself, with others and with one's creator.

E. *Marital Myths*

A marital myth is a fictitious belief about one's self, one's partner, or the relationship in general. One of the most persistent myths which individuals bring into marital therapy is, "If you really love me and I love you, everything will be fine and we will be intimate and close." Successful marriage and the development of an intimate relationship requires the effective development and use of relationship skills. These needed skills are seldom taught in the maturing years. Successful marriage does not occur "naturally" or by chance. The pastoral marital therapist must be able to teach these skills and coach client couples on their implementation so that the potentially destructive consequences of such myths can be avoided.

The greatest victim of the myth that "love conquers all" is couple communication. Disciplined practice of needed skills seldom occurs when couples adhere to this myth. In fact, such couples sometimes believe that if they must practice communication, then something must be "wrong" with the relationship or their love is deteriorating. Couples need to learn basic rules of communication such as the use of "I" messages, brevity of expression, and listening without judgment or criticism. Couples need to be able to distinguish between a reaction and a response and then practice responsive empathetic communication.

Parenting is another topic for education and discussion by the therapist. Couples sometimes believe that skilled parenting is a natural instinctive process and are deeply distressed when they experience the normal difficulties of raising children, or the normal feelings of at times not liking and resenting the children. Effective parenting requires many specific skills which should be taught by the pastoral marital therapist as needed. The marital relationship needs to be bounded and protected to facilitate growth of each individual and the entire family.

Good and lasting marriages do not happen by mistake or by chance. Both partners need to continually work at balancing all the demands on the individual, the couple and the family with the basics of what it takes for a marriage to be productive and growthful, i.e., time, communication, intimacy, sexuality, productivity, etc. The discovering, challenging, and correcting of each couple's marital myths can help facilitate this process.

Key Issues in Therapy

The pastoral marital therapist who embraces a philosophy of therapy consistent with these concepts must also come to grips with issues of balance, self-responsibility, process and content, systemic questions, enactments, and peer relationships.

A. *Balance*

In the practice of marital therapy there is perhaps no more important concept than balance. Because fault and responsibility are systemic in nature, both spouses need to acknowledge their individual contributions to a marital problem. The therapist's role is to orchestrate and protect a balanced approach which will allow both spouses to examine the "logs in their own eye" and not let one spouse project blame onto the other.

Balancing in marital therapy also is concerned with the amount of time and attribution of responsibility given to each spouse by the therapist. Working with or "on" one spouse for forty-five minutes of a fifty minute session constitutes an imbalance which can raise dynamics of one spouse feeling picked out as "the" problem, and the other partner feeling ignored or vindicated. Therapists who become imbalanced in approaching a couple often find one or both clients terminating therapy. Time, attention, confrontation, and support all need to be balanced by the therapist in his/her relationship to both partners.

The structure of therapy also needs to be balanced as much as possible. If a therapist was meeting with the wife of a couple for four sessions and then asked her husband to participate in the therapy, an imbalance has already occurred. Attempts to balance might be to include the husband from the outset of therapy, which is the most often preferred route, or, if this is not possible, to meet with the husband individually for several sessions before seeing the couple. There needs to be a continual attempt to balance the relationship that the therapist has with each spouse.

If the pastoral therapist loses a balanced approach, it may signify an issue of transference or counter-transference. If, for instance, a male therapist judges a woman for her domineering and aggressive personality and sides with her husband in order to protect him, there are clear transference issues for the therapist. One possibility is that the male therapist has had difficulty with his relationship with his mother and probably with assertiveness with women in general. Determination of whether the approach and attitudes of the therapist are balanced is one of the best assessment tools to determine how much help the therapist needs in dealing with the case.

Maintaining balance is a technique and a skill. Even though the therapist might understand the systemic nature of the couple's problems, balance can be lost due to a lack of ability to implement systems concepts within marital therapy. For example, a husband is confronted by the therapist for continually withdrawing from his wife. The therapist believes that in the next session he/she will confront the wife's complementary hostility. Unfortunately, in the intervening week the husband felt that he was being blamed and his wife reinforced this feeling when she said that she agreed with the therapist and wanted her husband to listen more closely. The couple never returned to therapy even though the wife felt that the therapist had done "a very good job." The skill of balancing the dynamics of a couple should be a continual topic of conversation in supervision.

B. Self-Responsibility

A major goal of the pastoral marital therapist is to teach self-responsibility to individuals and couples. This means that a great deal of the therapist's interventions are designed to help the couple see the complementary aspects of their marital difficulties. Sample questions that the therapist might ask are: "What is your part in the difficulty?" or "What is it that you do to escalate the problem?" Of course, in order to maintain balance, if one partner is asked these questions the other needs to be asked also and at relatively the same time, within five or ten minutes, or after the completion of the partner's response.

An individual who accepts part of the responsibility for the difficulties in the marriage increases his/her power to effect change. Unfortunately an individual most often tries to resolve the marital issues by trying to convince his/her spouse where he/she is in error. This creates, in the individual who is projecting responsibility, a great deal of frustration and feelings of being powerless. Client couples most often feel powerless because they are placing responsibility for change in the one place which is the most difficult to effect change, in their spouse. An individual has some ability to force change in another. A pastoral marital therapist will constantly seek to engender power by helping each person become self-responsible in the same spirit that Christ communicated when He said, "Let the one who is without sin cast the first stone."

C. Process and Content

The majority of beginning therapists get very confused, often frustrated, in working with couples because they pay far too much attention to the content the couple presents and fail to comprehend the process which characterizes their interactions. When Christ alluded to the importance of intention and matters of the heart over being able to say the "right" words he alluded to process dynamics as more important than content.

Content is the subject matter which a couple wants to present to the therapist. The couple will often want to share stories, arguments, and frustrations concerning children, work, time spent together, etc. Process considerations look behind this type of content and ask the questions as to why and in what manner the content is being communicated in the first place. Attention to process causes one to examine the depth and purpose of communication instead of the communication itself.

For example, a couple comes into therapy arguing about an event which happened six days ago. The therapist's approach was to listen to the content of the story and suggest some solutions to the problems. All of the therapist's interventions failed. While the content was clear to the therapist the process of the couple was not. The actual purpose of the story was to prevent the couple from having to have to talk intimately together within the session and in front of the therapist. By sharing the story with the therapist, the couple never had to talk to each other or truly share with one another how each felt or where each was hurting.

Examples of content questions are: "How old is she?" "Where did you go from there?" "How long did that last?" Process questions would look behind content to ask: "Why do you share that with me?" "Do you understand how you are saying that?" "What is the purpose of this argument?"

The "intimacy dance" is one of the most common process issues enacted by couples, and misunderstood by therapists. The couple, as most couples do, have fears of being intimate and vulnerable. To protect themselves, they develop a dance with prescribed steps and movements to protect their own vulnerabilities. For instance, in order to not be vulnerable, a spouse will start a fight, stay longer hours at work, or constantly invite a friend over to the house. The other spouse, to complete the dance, will ignore and distance himself/herself from the partner. If the therapist decides to ask the spouse to come home earlier, as the main intervention, both partners will most likely resist and collude together by simply replacing work with another distancing technique. The key for the therapist is to enable the couple to understand the dance and the underlying fears so that the process can be confronted by them and reconciliation can occur through understanding, changed behaviors by both partners, and increased intimacy.

D. *Systemic Questions*

There is a difference between systemic and linear questions. A linear question would seek to understand the cause or the person responsible for a certain difficulty. With a couple, if the wife was angry, the therapist might ask, in a linear fashion, "How long have you felt angry?" or "Where does your anger come from?" Linear questions look for understanding from an individualistic perspective. Systemic questions seek to discover the interrelatedness of behavior. In systemic understanding, it is assumed that behavior in one spouse is somehow related to behavior in the other. Systemic questions point out shared responsibility. For example, a husband believes that his wife is unloving and uncaring. Judgmentally, he points to his wife as the problem, and the therapist, losing all sense of balance, agrees with the husband. If the therapist asked a linear question of the wife such as "What prevents you from being more loving?" the wife will most likely feel judged and abused. If the pastoral therapist regains some systemic sense of fairness and mutual responsibility, he/she will perhaps ask a systemic question such as "How do you help your wife be so distant from you?" or "What do you do to elicit her response?" Of course this systemic question could not be asked unless there was a balancing question for the wife, such as, "How do you contribute to your husband's judgmental attitude?" Examples of other systemic questions are: "What is your part of the problem?"; "How do you prevent your spouse from caring for you?"; "What is it about your behavior which affects your spouse?" These types of questions need to be asked in a balanced way, with sensitivity, and with the therapist's conviction that both partners are contributing to the dysfunction of the system.

E. *Enactments*

Enactments are conversations or role plays which the therapist orchestrates to understand and improve the couple's manner of relating to each other. Many therapists, most often out of their own need to control, feel that they need to be the center of attention. One consequence is that they do not let a couple interact with one another within the therapeutic session. In such cases most conversation is directed to the therapist. This can increase the dependence of the couple and prevent them from learning how to speak to one another. A therapist who needs to be central will spend considerable time listening to, and being empathetic with, each partner's hurt and frustration. A pastoral marital therapist, instead of monopolizing the empathy, should teach each partner to be empathic and caring of the spouse's feelings. Consequently, dependence and transference onto the pastoral therapist is much less of an emphasis, and the couple learns to care for each other.

Enactments redirect the conversation so that the couple is encouraged to talk to each other. In setting up a communication enactment the therapist might, along with other suggestions, ask a couple to face each other, refer to one's spouse in the first person not the third, speak in the present tense, and share a current feeling, not one felt two weeks ago. The therapist's role then becomes one of focusing the couple's communication, teaching communication skills, and helping each partner develop an increased capacity to be vulnerable and receptive to the other.

Enactments as an intervention, and partner communication as a goal, are often more difficult concepts for the pastor who was trained in a tradition in which church hierarchy and dogma are more prevalent. In such traditions, the pastor is a more central figure in the communication of the congregant with God and it is often difficult for him/her to step out of this central role in a couple's communication.

F. Peer Relationships

A common process issue in marital therapy is the inability of a couple to relate to each other at a peer level. Both spouses, based on fear or insecurity, often attempt to, in some manner, act inferior or superior toward the other. In such a dynamic the peer relationship and the potentials for intimacy are lost and dysfunctional dynamics can ensue.

A common reason for the loss of the peer relationship is that individuals consciously and/or unconsciously become a parent or child to the other. Mother-son and father-daughter dynamics between spouses hurt all aspects of the intimate relationship. Such dynamics occur when, for instance, a wife asks her husband to do something and the husband resists, or when a husband gives his wife an order and she passively ignores him. These dynamics are reminiscent of a parent's relationship to a rebellious teenager.

The pastoral therapist should continually ask the process question, "Is this couple speaking and relating to each other as peers, or are they in some manner one up or one down in relation to the other?" This dynamic is very common because of its strong correlation with the parent-child relationship each spouse often has with his/her parents. Most often, if a forty year old "child" feels like a child in relationship to his/her parents, similar dynamics will appear in the marriage. A lack of differentiation in family of origin often results in a similar lack in the marital relationship.

Couple Dynamics

Other systems concepts which the pastoral marital therapist needs to understand and utilize include homeostasis, complementarity, and the merging of the past and the present.

A. *Homeostasis*

Homeostatic principles suggest that systems are often very difficult to change due to built-in forces which resist movement. Because a system is not linearly but collectively controlled, the movement of any one person can often be counteracted by the movement of someone else and the status quo maintained. For example, in a marriage, one spouse decides to do something about the boredom he/she feels every weekend, but the other partner resists. An argument then ensues which causes both partners to throw up their hands in disgust, with the result being that nothing actually is done differently. The homeostatic balance was restored. Couples will often go to great lengths to maintain the status quo because, even though it is painful or they are dissatisfied, the dynamics they are experiencing are ones which they can predict and are probably ones which protect them from more fearful insecurities.

Homeostatic principles are important for the pastoral marital therapist to understand for several reasons. First, a therapist's expectation that change will always occur quickly can be placed into a more realistic perspective. Second, the therapist's understanding of the resilience of marital systems will allow him/her to be less likely to believe a couple who says they are giving up and heading for divorce. In such a case, a therapist can prematurely stop investing in a couple if he/she is not aware of general resistance to change. Often, individuals will speak of what they intend to do, but the homeostasis of the system prevents it. In other words, as one partner moves forward affectionately, the other moves back out of fear; or as soon as one partner threatens to leave the relationship, the other becomes more loving and conciliatory, taking away some of the energy needed for the other partner to leave in the first place. Unfortunately, these dances and reciprocal behaviors which maintain homeostasis within a couple can get very organized over time. This increasing organization is called negentropy, the increased patterning and organization of a system the longer it works together.

B. Complementarity

This systems concept has been alluded to for years in such folk wisdom as "opposites attract." Complementarity is seen in the balance couples achieve in finding a spouse who will exemplify qualities of behavior which are opposite to, or augment in some manner, their own. A woman who tends to be more emotional will tend to marry someone who is more withdrawn or cognitive. A man who is dominant and insecure will often marry a woman who is more passive, but quietly in control. Individuals often find partners who complement their own deficencies, as, for example, the success- and task-oriented spouse who finds a partner who lives more in the day to day emotions.

Knowledge of complementarity helps the therapist to understand the balances which couples attain. In the best scenarios, the therapist can point out the strengths of each partner and what they have to offer the other. The complementary relationship will be worked with in hopes of making each individual more whole through an intimate relationship with the spouse. The thinking oriented husband can be taught, within the relationship to his emotional wife, to begin to feel, and vice versa.

Unfortunately, while complementary relationships offer the potential for each partner to grow more completely and more whole, they also create the potential for polarization. Many couples who come into therapy, instead of growing in the relationship to the other, have become more rigidly defended in their own particular personality traits and styles. Through a process called circular causality, each partner's behavior creates a reaction in the other which creates a greater reaction and so on and so on. In a circular fashion, fears and inabilities get more entrenched. Referring to the example given above, the husband cannot relate to his wife emotionally. His wife gets angrier and angrier, which increases the fear of the husband who has, as his greatest defense, the ability to think. The more he obsesses, the more she emotes and vice versa. These dynamics increase in a circular fashion until there is some ventilation, a cooling off period, and the beginning again of the circular pattern. In such a couple thinking and emotion can become polarized to the extent that the husband seemingly represses all feeling and the wife forgets how to think.

Another classic example occurs in the dynamics of strength and weakness. A "strong" male marries a perceived "weak" female. He, being afraid of his weakness, criticizes and judges his wife, thus increasing her feelings of being weak and unable. She, in turn, projects all of her power onto her husband, helping him to feel powerful. Before long, both parties actually believe their assigned roles. Interestingly, these seemingly strong and weak relationships often do a complete reversal later in the marriage or after a divorce. In this case the woman is able to grow in her self-concept, and her increased power so threatens the male that he is confronted with his own impotence which his wife will no longer carry and protect for him.

All relationships are complementary in some fashion. It is part of the pastoral marital therapist's role to encourage each spouse to learn from the other and integrate those qualities which are carried in the spouse but yet to be integrated in the self. If the complementary aspects of the relationship polarize, both individuals of the marriage are less able to grow and develop.

C. Merging the Past and the Present

While traditional individual psychotherapy lays considerable emphasis on past experiences and related emotional feelings, marital and systemic therapy consists more of a merging of the past and the present. In a systemic approach the pastoral therapist will listen for the present feelings, experiences, and communications of a couple and often relate them back to the past and specifically the family of origin. After rooting and labeling these feelings in the past, sometimes eliciting the feelings within the session, the systemic therapist would often aid in the clients' assessment of how these feelings are contributing to the couple's communication and circular patterns of relating to one another in the present. Thus a feeling shared by one partner would both be rooted in the past and also related to the dynamics of the present couple interaction. In each session this diving into the past and relating the feeling to the present will often occur. Balance in approach, eliciting emotion and relating the emotion to the past and the present in both partners is very important.

In working with emotions systemically, one of the primary tools of the pastoral marital therapist is to listen for "historical statements" expressed by both clients. Historical statements are ones which are imbedded in everyday couple communication and speak to an earlier and more powerful emotional history on the topic being discussed. Such statements are often characterized by the use of absolutes. For example, the expression of one partner to another, "You always reject me," probably describes not only some of the marital dynamics but also an earlier emotional history of feelings of rejection. Another partner states, "You never have respected me!" similarly describes certain marital dynamics as well as a poor self-concept in the expressor.

Another pattern which reveals the true intensity of feeling and suggests a need for the pastoral therapist to relate the emotion to history occurs when the intensity of a response does not seemingly match the intention of the expression. For example, a wife states, "Honey, I'm sorry I forgot our anniversary," and the husband responds, "You have never loved me!"

Merging the past and the present is an important role for the systemically oriented pastoral therapist. Most therapy would be characterized by a continual relating of present feeling to the historical roots and then back to the present for an examination of relational implications.

Family Dynamics

Individuals are not only part of a marital system or a nuclear family system composed of a husband, wife, and children. They are also part of a larger and broader system which includes parents and grandparents, brothers and sisters, aunts, uncles, and cousins. Many generations impact upon each individual as the marvelous intergenerational narrative of Abraham, Isaac, and Jacob in Genesis demonstrated. Issues of boundaries, alignments, enmeshment, emotional cut-off, triangulation, legacy, and introjection and projection leap from the Biblical pages as living reminders of issues that each marriage and family and every therapist must understand and work to resolve.

A. *Boundaries*

One basic assumption of marital and family theory is that boundaries are very important. Three types of boundaries which need to be considered are intergenerational, structural, and marital.

Intergenerational boundaries are intended to separate and define the different generations of a family. For instance, in terms of power and responsibility is it clear who are the parents, who are the grandparents, and who are the children? Often marital couples will come to therapy in chaos because their children are in effect functional parents, more powerful and in control than the actual parents themselves. Other similar boundary problems occur when the grandparents parent their grandchildren and diminish the effectiveness of the real parents. An assumption in marital therapy is that the clearer the boundaries are between the generations the more a couple has the ability to form and nurture a sound marriage.

Structural boundaries are concrete objects or agreed upon rules that separate people from one another. Structural questions might include inquiries into the use of doors, open or shut, knocking before entering, who has keys, the thickness of walls, etc. Questions might include: "Do the children knock on the parents' bedroom door before entering, or do they just walk in?" or "Do the grandparents have a key to their children's homes and do they enter without knocking?" Without structural boundaries, a marriage can be greatly invaded and undermined. If children, parents, or friends of the couple can enter the marital relationship at will, it is difficult for marital partners to not feel jealous, competitive, or simply exhausted.

Marital boundaries refer specifically to whether a couple will defend the time and the privacy of the relationship. Work, pressures, children, etc., all need to be boundaried at times so that the couple can build and enrich the marriage. Does the couple go out alone together? Can they talk privately within their own house even if there are children present in the home? The pastoral marital therapist, before beginning with some complicated assessment or intervention needs to determine how much of the couple's difficulties are caused by the lack of maintenance of sufficient boundaries surrounding the marital relationship.

B. Alignments

Alignments are special relationships between people in the family, usually involving the exclusion of someone else. It is hoped, for instance, that the marital couple is aligned and to some degree the children and remainder of the family are in a flexible and appropriate manner "boundaried out." However, more often than not, in marriages that are experiencing difficulty, the alignments are not between the husband and the wife but between one of the spouses and a child, a friend, or a parent, the result being that one of the spouses is excluded. Many dynamics contribute to the formation of alignments. One of the most common is unresolved loyalties, strong emotional attachments, to a parent which can cause a forty year old "child" to consider the opinion or the emotions of that parent before and above those of the spouse. Equally frequent is the alignment of a parent and a child, which for the parent can be an attempt to attain love, affection, or a sense of power which he/she does not feel within the marital relationship.

C. Enmeshment and Emotional Cut-Off

Enmeshment and emotional cut-off are key dynamics in most couples who come for therapy. Two partners who are enmeshed are poorly differentiated and unable to defend and boundary their own identity and personality. In the marital relationship, such people often regress at times of crisis or difficulty. Emotions become paramount in enmeshed relationships and the ability to be objective, respectful and considerate is diminished. Individuals almost always become enmeshed when they marry before each of their identities is sufficiently formed. This causes very basic insecurities in the relationship such as rejection, abandonment, and feelings of being smothered or overwhelmed. Such couples are often judgmental.

A parent and a child can be enmeshed. When the child cannot emotionally separate from a parent he/she feels emotions similar to those noted above, and the attitudes of the parents often overwhelm the thought processes of the child. While some of these feelings would be normal for a young child, for an enmeshed parent and an eighteen year old child such a situation is far from "normal." Such enmeshment affects the child's ability to mature, and often leads to acting out behavior which disrupts the marital relationship.

Emotional cut-off seems to be the opposite of enmeshment but is, in actuality, one aspect of it. A father and son, for example, who are emotionally cut-off, haven't spoken to each other for five years. The energy it takes not to speak to the other, the anger, hatred, fear, etc., keeps the two people inextricably intertwined and emotionally bonded. A spouse who is emotionally cut-off from a child or a parent is carrying a considerable amount of anger which often creates difficulty within the marriage.

D. Triangulation

When a couple is enmeshed there are many attempts, usually counterproductive, to separate sufficiently to gain back one's individual identity. Couples will become angry as an attempt to gain back power and create distance, but in so doing actually become more enmeshed in the relationship. Another attempt to establish some sort of separation is called triangulation. An enmeshed couple will triangulate a third party, most often a child, into the relationship to both provide some distance and remove the fears of having to be intimate. With the presence of a triangulated figure fears of intimacy can be hidden and avoided. Other possibilities to be triangulated into an enmeshed relationship are a friend, parent, work, alcohol, hobbies, etc.

E. Legacy

Family legacies are powerful themes and emotions which characterize the historical dynamics of a family. The legacies which each spouse brings into the relationship are very significant for the well functioning or poor functioning of the marriage. A family legacy might take the form of what a child is expected or entitled to become, i.e., four generations of the family have all gone to the same college or worked at the same profession. Other legacies might concern where and in what style one should live, how much a person should enjoy life or experience pleasure, or dynamics having to do with morals or ethics handed down from one generation to the next. If an individual attempts to break one of these legacies and becomes disloyal, such as marrying out of one's faith, great feelings of guilt and anxiety can occur. The understanding of the differing legacies of each spouse and how they might contradict each other is often an important aspect of marital therapy.

F. Introjection and Projection

Introjection is a process by which a very young child incorporates into himself/herself the attitudes, emotions, understandings, and habits experienced in relationship with both parents. Sometimes these introjects can be very discordant. A violent father creates fear in his son. The son introjects both the violence and the fear of being hurt by violence into his growing sense of self. The introject becomes both the violence and the related fear. What happens in marriages is that such early introjects are reawakened, exacerbated and repetitively played out through the projection of part of the introject onto one's spouse.

Conclusion

A sound conceptual background is a necessity for the pastoral marital therapist who wants to truly effect change and promote growth in a couple. A marriage that is spiritually alive consists of two people who seek continual growth and development of the relationship. In order to promote change the pastor or lay leader needs to assess not only possible dysfunction, but also the strengths of a couple. Often relational difficulty can be a precursor for constructive change. If the pastoral therapist is rooted in the possibilities instead of the negatives such change can often take place.

Differentiation and reconciliation are the rudders of the marital voyage. The ability for each spouse to separate while remaining connected to the family of origin is crucial for the quality of the marital interaction. In a more differentiated state the individual can be more compassionate, caring, and patient with all the complexities of the spouse's personality and couple dynamics.

As a framework for the practice of pastoral marital therapy certain concepts are key. A balanced approach in terms of time and attribution of responsibility is crucial if one partner or the other is not going to feel judged or, conversely, guilt free. Balance is essential for a systemic approach. Process issues need to be weighed at least as heavily as the content presented by the couple. The intent of a communication either conscious or unconscious is more powerful and responded to more completely than content. Systemic questions can quickly confront process issues which are destructive for the couple. A systemic question will assist an individual's understanding of how his/her behavior is affecting his/her spouse. Finally, true assessment of differentiation, balance and process issues is best accomplished when the pastoral therapist orchestrates enactments for couple communication within the therapeutic hour.

Marital interaction is guided by a number of systemic principles. Two of the foremost are homeostasis and complementarity. Homeostasis describes the self-regulation of a system in maintaining the status quo. The pastoral marital therapist perhaps can replace anger or impatience over the lack of a couple's movement with more creative intervention if homeostatic principles are acknowledged. Understanding of complementarity in marital choice and couple communication patterns will allow for reconciliation in place of polarization within the marital dyad.

The extended family system and the structures within it are important for the pastoral therapist's understanding of the interactions of the couple. Boundaries between people and generations allow for differentiation instead of enmeshment. Alignments between family members, especially those which exclude certain people, need to be examined and confronted. Emotional cut-off and the consequent internalization of anger and guilt should be highlighted and moved toward reconciliation. Triangulation patterns need to be discovered and confronted to increase the potential for intimacy. In all of the above the loyalties and legacies of the individuals and family need to be uncovered in that they provide an emotional map for the future of the marital dyad.

A conceptual understanding of theories and concepts from a number of systemic schools will ensure that the pastoral marital therapist will not be engaging in the practice of marital therapy without any basic understanding or therapeutic skills.

Reference

Luthman, S. *The Dynamic Family*. Palo Alto: Science Behavior Books, 1974.

For Further Reading

Berman, E., Lief, H., & Williams, A.M. "A Model of Marital Interaction." In G.P. Sholevar (ed.), *The Handbook of Marriage and Marital Therapy* (pp. 3–34). New York: SP Medical & Scientific Books, 1981.

Framo, J. "The Integration of Marital Therapy with Sessions with Family of Origin." In A.S. Gurman and D.P. Kniskern (eds.), *Handbook of Family Therapy* (pp. 133–158). New York: Brunner/Mazel, 1981.

Framo, J. "Family of Origin as a Therapeutic Resource for Adults in

Marital and Family Therapy: You Can and Should Go Home Again." *Family Process, 15*(2), 193–210, 1976.

Frank, C. (1984). "Contextual Family Therapy." *American Journal of Therapy, 12*(1), 3–6, 1984.

Gurman, A., Kniskern, D. (eds.). *Handbook of Family Therapy.* New York: Brunner/Mazel, 1981. **An encyclopedia of marital and family theory with clinical applications.**

Kerr, M.E. "Family Systems Theory and Therapy." In A.S. Gurman and D.P. Kniskern (eds.), *Handbook of Family Therapy* (pp. 226–264). New York: Brunner/Mazel, 1981.

L'Abate, L. (ed.). *The Handbook of Family Psychology & Therapy, Vol. I.* Illinois: Dorsey, 1985. **Encyclopedia of family therapy perspectives.**

L'Abate, L. (ed.). *The Handbook of Family Psychology & Therapy, Vol. II.* Illinois: Dorsey, 1985.

L'Abate, L., & McHenry, S. *Handbook of Marital Interventions.* New York: Grune & Stratton, 1983.

Minuchin, S. *Families and Family Therapy.* Cambridge, MA: Harvard University Press, 1974. **A book on structural family therapy.**

Resnikoff, R.O. "Teaching Family Therapy: Ten Key Questions for Understanding the Family as Patient." *Journal of Marital and Family Therapy, 7,* 135–142.

Sager, C.J. "Marital Contracts." In G.P. Sholevar (ed.), *The Handbook of Marriage and Marital Therapy* (pp. 35–76). New York: SP Medical & Scientific Books, 1981.

Chapter 4

The Tasks of the Therapist in the
Counseling Process: Part I

The pastor involved in doing effective marital counseling is required to have a great number of personal and interpersonal skills. As the counseling process unfolds, there are five tasks that are particularly salient for the pastor to accomplish: *listen effectively; assess accurately; develop flexible treatment plans; develop and utilize a variety of intervention techniques; use one's self effectively.* To the extent that these tasks are accomplished in the counseling process, the likelihood is increased that the skills of the pastoral minister will be used to their greatest potential and that productive counseling will occur.

In this first of two chapters which address the tasks of the therapist in the counseling process, the focus is upon the first two tasks: the need to listen effectively and the need to assess accurately.

1. Listen Effectively

Perhaps the greatest gift that the pastoral marital therapist can give to those who are counseled is the gift of total listening. In an increasingly technologically oriented and impersonal society, many people feel lonely and isolated, cut-off from one of the most necessary ingredients for personal and human growth, namely, intimate dialogue in which each person truly hears the message of the other person. Many marital partners experience this sense of isolation and loneliness, as hurt and angry feelings are accumulated, as conflicts are ignored or mishandled, as alienation and doubts invade a relationship in which the foundations of trust, love and commitment are being somewhat attacked or eroded by a variety of forces within and without the marriage. Many of these people seek out their pastor or a pastoral counselor to enable them to overcome the alienation, and to create stronger marital bonds and a deeper relationship with their partner. For most, the ability to listen effectively is woefully under-developed, and without it significant change is virtually impossible.

There are many reasons why people do not develop the ability to listen effectively. Many of us are too concerned with making our own point or defeating the other person. Some of us rely too much on rationality and logic, and refuse to attend to the affective or emotional side of ourselves or others. Others of us are just the opposite; we rely so much on how we feel that we fail to attend to our own or others' thoughts and rational processes. So often, the counselor hears statements such as "He/she is so rational!" or "He/she is just too emotional!" All of these block the ability to genuinely listen.

If the counselor is to enable the couple to develop effective listening skills, he/she must have them and model them. There must be self-awareness of one's own feelings, thoughts and behaviors, so that delineation and differentiation can occur between oneself and the other person. Genuine empathy or sensitivity to the other person is also required, a sense that is communicated to the other person that the listener hears, understands and shares in the words, feelings and experience of the presenter. This is demonstrated through maintaining eye contact, the use of a caring voice tone, reflecting back what was heard to confirm understanding, asking open-ended questions which probe for deeper meaning, the lack of critical judgments, and the use of statements which demonstrate acceptance, such as "I understand," or "That must have been painful for you."

The counselor must also be able to be sensitive to his/her own feelings which occur in response to the actions, words or feelings of the presenter, which some counselors refer to as "recipathy." In addition, the counselor must be aware of, and sensitive to, the impact of his/her own words and actions upon the persons being counseled. All of these are components of effective listening.

The counselor must be able to listen totally, with one's whole self, to the other person. Such listening involves being totally attentive to all of the cues being sent by the person, listening with one's ears, eyes, mind, heart, imagination, and even appropriate touch. Attention must be given to what is being said verbally and non-verbally, and to what is not being said, such as hidden or unexpressed feelings, which might only be alluded to by a downcast look or a slight change in voice tone or inflection. As noted above, it involves listening to many dimensions of one's self as well.

When such listening occurs in an atmosphere in which genuine warmth and caring is present, in which unconditional positive regard and non-judgmental acceptance (not to be confused with unqualified approval) is present, genuine support can be experienced. In such an atmosphere, those being counseled get a sense of the universality of the human condition, the universality of hurt and angry feelings, success, failures, forgiveness, and reconciliation. They experience the reality of physical and psychological availability to each other, and the possibility of interactions that are congruent and based on trust in one's self and the other person. From this can develop the ability to appropriately recognize the contributions of one's own behavior and those of one's partner to the successes and failures of the marital relationship. When this occurs, genuine and integrated change becomes a distinct possibility. But without genuine listening, without the sense that one is cared for enough to be heard by the counselor and by one's partner, defensive postures must be maintained to protect the self.

The Gospels are filled with examples of how the listening of Jesus impacted upon those around him. Behind the words of the Samaritan woman he heard her inadequacies and difficulties with commitment, and reflected them back to her, preparing the way for a new life. In discussions with Nicodemus he heard the genuine search for meaning, but also the fears which caused him to come at night to speak with Jesus. The Master sensed that Nicodemus could not get beyond the literal meaning of his words, perhaps out of fear of the changes that would be required of him. But, sensitive to those fears, Jesus directed him to a new life.

In the story of the woman caught in adultery, we see the listening of Jesus at its best. Confronted with a mob bent on condemning a woman, but also bent on trapping him, Jesus just listened to their rantings and ravings. Instead of responding to the "bait" or the challenge, he heard their rage, their indignation, and their resentments. Instead of responding to their attempt to place him in a double-bind (if he followed the Law and permitted her to be stoned, he would have been perceived as uncaring; if he told them to let her go, he would have been perceived as not upholding the Law—either way he would lose), he turned the issue back upon them with the request that the one of them that was without sin should cast the first stone. We could say that that was a calculated gamble on his part, but we could also say that he listened very attentively to the non-verbal messages of the people in the crowd, and "heard" the aspects of them that were responsive and receptive to a new way to hear the Law. Then, when left alone with the woman, he heard her non-verbal awe and shame, and declared that he was not there to condemn her, sending her away to a new life with clear instructions not to commit that sin again.

In these and other examples, it is abundantly clear that Jesus was a master at total listening. In his meditation and prayer life, it was clear that he experienced God listening to him. Out of that spiritual intimacy with his Father came the roots of his ability to develop the skills of effective listening. Paul wrote that God helps or comforts us, so that we can be able to help and comfort those who experience troubles of any kind, using the same help and comfort the he has given us (2 Corinthians 1:3–4). God listens! Jesus listened! The pastoral counselor must also be an effective listener to enable the couples who seek help to develop the listening skills which are vital to their development of genuine intimacy and integrated and permanent change within their marital relationship.

The first task then of the therapist in the counseling process is the sine qua non, the absolute prerequisite of effective marital counseling or therapy: listen effectively.

2. Assess Accurately

If we assume that the pastoral marital therapist has developed the ability to listen effectively, and does so, he/she is then left with the question of what to do with what has been "heard" verbally and non-verbally. A determination must be made regarding what is significant and what is insignificant, what is of primary importance and what is secondary, and what must be responded to immediately versus what can be put off to another place and time. To answer these questions, the counselor must do an accurate assessment of the marital relationship of the couple who have come for counseling.

The first requirement for doing such an assessment of the marital relationship is to think systemically. Historically, most of us have been trained to think in terms of cause and effect relationships, with A causing B; in other words, to think linearly. Systemic thinking requires the ability to think in a circular fashion, with A impacting upon B, but B also impacting upon A, while both impact upon and are impacted by C, D, E, and so forth.

Every marriage is composed of a variety of sub-systems, such as the couple, children, extended family, each individual, bio-medical, religio-ethical, social, etc. Each of these sub-systems impacts upon the marital relationship and is in turn impacted by it and a variety of other forces. As the counselor assesses the interrelationship of these complex patterns within and upon the marital relationship, the temptation must be avoided to focus upon the apparently obvious and apparently "easy" linear aspects of the relationship.

Such a comprehensive and systemic evaluation of the marriage allows the therapist to gain a broad overview of forces within and outside the relationship which have contributed to the development and maintenance of marital strengths and problems. In addition, the counselor is able to identify a host of forces which can be utilized to help enhance and support the marital relationship, while at the same time identifying those which might inhibit or block relationship change, adjustment or growth.

The assessment process that is being described here is an ongoing process, and is not limited to the information gathered in the first few sessions. The treatment plan is based upon the initial assessment, but as that plan unfolds, the assessment process continues, with confirmations and disconfirmations of initial hypotheses. The treatment plan is then affirmed, revised, modified, tuned, or changed dramatically as the ongoing assessment process continues. In short, assessment effects treatment, but treatment effects assessment, and so on.

This assessment process is also done with the active participation of the client couple, and is not just done by the counselor. Who else knows the relationship better? They live it! The interaction between a couple genuinely seeking help and a knowledgeable counselor permits the identification and exploration of the subtle and not so subtle dimensions of the relationship that have led these people to this point in their marital life. Such an open and active process, which involves all parties working together as a team, does a lot to facilitate insight in each partner, diminish anxiety, and instill hope as they plan and work together toward a common goal of relationship enhancement and positive change. Pastoral counselors must avoid the temptation to believe that they know what is best for those seeking help, as well as the temptation to keep the assessment process and the development of the subsequent goals almost exclusively in their own hands.

An effective assessment of a marital relationship includes at least five areas of focus: (1) inventories which assess marital adjustment and satisfaction, and which help identify individual and marital strengths and areas of potential problems or growth or change; (2) each individual's personality style and development; (3) the current relationship style of the couple; (4) the original and current marital contract; (5) the extended family and life cycle issues.

A. Inventories

There are a host of inventories available to the pastoral marital counselor which identify a host of things, from marital satisfaction and adjustment, to individual personality variables and styles, to relationship strengths and potential work areas. The use of such inventories, especially if they are statistically reliable and valid, can be a great asset to the counselor. They can provide a wealth of diagnostic information to the couple and therapist alike, confirming or disconfirming initial impressions, and providing information in areas that might have been initially overlooked or avoided by the counselor. The beginning counselor especially can proceed with greater confidence, with the assurance of some objective underpinnings to the assessment and counseling process.

A description of all of the excellent available inventories would take an inordinate amount of space and time. However, one instrument found to be reliable and valid and especially useful is *PRE-PARE/ENRICH*. There are three inventories contained in this package: ENRICH (Evaluation and Nurturing Relationship Issues, Communication and Happiness) is designed for couples seeking marital counseling or enrichment; PREPARE (PREmarital Personal and Relationship Evaluation) is designed to help couples prepare for marriage; and, PREPARE—MC (PREmarital Personal and Relationship Evaluation—Marriage with Children) is designed to help couples who already have children to prepare for marriage.

The inventories are filled out by each partner, sent off to be computer scored, and a profile for each partner is returned, indicating relationship strengths and potential work areas and how these might impact upon a marital relationship. The profile provides the couple with an excellent vehicle for communicating about significant personal and relationship issues. The discussion can be an opportunity for genuinely learning about oneself and building intimacy with one's partner. In addition, as the participant-observer counselor facilitates the discussion, diagnostic functions can be served as well.

A detailed description of each of these inventories is beyond the scope of this chapter, but several of the areas addressed are the following: realistic expectations, personality issues, communication, conflict résolution, financial management, leisure activities, sexual relationship, children and marriage, family and friends, egalitarian roles, religious orientation, idealistic distortion, marital satisfaction, marital cohesion or togetherness, and marital adaptabity and change.

(These inventories can be purchased from Prepare-Enrich, Inc., P.O. Box 190, Minneapolis, MN 55440, Phone: 612-331-1661). Some training is required to use these inventories, and it can be secured through participation in one of the workshops which are held periodically across the country, or through self-instruction materials which can also be purchased.)

The reliable and valid nature of these instruments, the fact that the norms are constantly updated, the focus on strengths and potential work areas, the personal and relationship focus, the ease of administration, the computer scoring, the readable profile and the concrete guidelines for feedback and discussion lead us to highly recommend the use of the PREPARE/ENRICH materials in the assessment process.

B. Individual Development and Personality Styles

Although the primary focus of pastoral marital counseling is the marital relationship itself, the counselor must still be well acquainted with personality development theory and psychopathology. The forces which contribute to the formation of each individual lead to the development of personality variables and a personality style which directly affects the way an individual relates to other people and to the world around him/her. Needless to say, such variables and styles impact greatly upon a marital relationship and the quality of interaction experienced therein.

Clifford Sager (1976) has done a great deal of relatively recent work developing personality typologies and discussing how they interact in marital relationships. His discussion of parent, child, romantic, rational, companionate, parallel and equal partner styles has provided helpful guidelines for clinicians desirous of blending individual personality theory with marital theory and counseling. However, even an in-depth awareness of his typologies is no substitute for substantive study in the area of personality development.

The pastoral marital counselor must also have a knowledge of individual psychopathology, so that he/she may be aware of significant individual issues which are impacting upon the marital relationship. Familiarity with the *Diagnostic and Statistical Manual of Mental Disorders—(DSM-III)* will give the counselor knowledge of the diagnostic criteria of the various forms of emotional illness. With such knowledge, the counselor can be able to at least preliminarily assess the nature and severity of individual issues which are presented to him/her, e.g., chronic anxiety, mood disorder, thought disorder, personality disorder, etc. This will increase the likelihood that the pastoral marital counselor will work within the areas and bounds of his/her training, expertise and experience, and not get in over his/her head or "walk where angels fear to tread." If the assessment process reveals significant psychopathology, referral to a qualified clinician for further assessment and/or treatment is indicated.

C. *The Current Relationship Style of the Couple*

As the counselor assesses the relationship style of the couple, he/she discovers forces within the relationship which can facilitate or inhibit growth and change. Consideration is given to several key questions:

- How do the partners handle their membership, power/control and intimacy needs within this marriage?
- How do they balance feelings, thoughts and actions?
- How effective are their communication processes?
- How effectively do they solve problems and make decisions?
- How effectively do they manage conflict?

Membership, power/control and intimacy needs. In every relationship, it is essential that each partner have a sense of positive self-identity as well as a sense of belonging and commitment to the partner and the marital relationship. Where self-identity or self-esteem is deficient, or where the partners are committed to each other or the relationship at different levels, problems often arise.

Some people are comfortable with a higher degree of individuation or disengagement than others. Some are comfortable with a higher degree of togetherness or enmeshment. The counselor's task is to assess each person's needs in this area, the level of self-esteem in each partner, the extent of commitment to the partner and the relationship, and the nature of the commitment, e.g., is it out of genuine love and care, or out of a sense of duty, obligation or guilt?

When partners have vastly different needs in these areas, strong fears can emerge, fears of being "swallowed up" or fears of being abandoned. Such fears can erode trust, and decrease the likelihood of being willing to be self-disclosing, vulnerable or intimate, leading to increasing distance to protect oneself or to aggressive attacks to get the spouse to come closer or to drive him/her away to avoid further pain. The counselor's task in such cases is to facilitate the development of sufficient self-identify and self-esteem and to enable the couple to develop somewhat similar levels of commitment to each other and the relationship. When this occurs, the possibilities for effective marital functioning, change, intimacy, and marital counseling increase dramatically.

With regard to power or control issues, each partner needs to have a sense of personal power and responsibility, and a sense that he/she can influence the direction and quality of the relationship. In addition, the partner must be viewed as an appropriately powerful and responsible person. The counselor assesses how the power is distributed in the relationship, how roles are agreed upon or negotiated, and how decisions are made. The focus is on such issues as the following: Does one person "rule the roost," or is power equally distributed? Does one partner make all or most of the decisions, exercising arbitrary veto power? Does one partner control through the inappropriate use of feelings or rationality? Can each partner take the "lead" in the relationship, when needed? Does each partner work for compromise or decisions by unanimous consent?

If one partner feels "powerful," and the other feels "powerless," the stage is set for serious conflict. Frequently, the "powerful" partner gets tired "carrying" the "weak" spouse, and the "weak" or "powerless" spouse gets tired of being dominated by the "powerful" or "strong" partner. What frequently arises is a series of overt and covert, active and passive, power or control gambits which destroy intimacy and increase pain and alienation. What is needed is for each person to feel and be powerful and responsible and to perceive the partner in the same way. In such a situation, creative problem solving and shared power and responsibility are likely to occur.

When the pastoral marital counselor looks at the issue of intimacy, closeness and distance needs are being assessed. Intimacy is defined here as prolonged closeness with another person, seeing each other as we really are, without any masks or games, characterized by openness, trust, affection, and the sharing of deep aspects of ourself with our partner. Intimacy can be experienced in a variety of forms: emotional, sexual, creative, aesthetic, work, recreational, intellectual, crisis, spiritual, and so forth. Since it is impossible to be intimate with everyone in every way, each of us must choose with whom we want to be intimate and in what ways, and then work intentionally to achieve those types and levels of intimacy.

The counselor needs to assess the extent to which each partner is happy with the types and quality of intimacy experienced in the relationship, and to enable them to define and work toward attainment of the types and quality they each desire. When one or both partners feel unfulfilled in a particular area of intimacy which is defined as necessary, the potential for pain, resentment and alienation is obvious.

Feelings, thoughts and actions. If individuals or relationships are to fulfill their potential, there must be a healthy balance between feelings, thoughts and actions. Partners must be able to experience and express effectively and appropriately the full range of human emotions: the highs and the lows, the joy and the sadness, the happiness and the anger, the contentment and the resentments, the fears and the hopes, the love and the loneliness. Partners must also be able to express their thoughts to each other clearly and rationally, without cognitive distortions or irrational beliefs.

In many relationships, one partner is the "thinker" and the other the "feeler," with one side of the personality so underdeveloped that each partner is attracted to the missing piece of the self that is seen in the partner. Yet, because it is also a disowned and feared piece of the self, each partner is simultaneously attracted and repelled by the other. In such relationships, cognitive distortions and irrational beliefs are frequently rampant. Negative aspects of the relationship are frequently over-magnified, while significant positives or strengths are minimized or discounted. Over-generalizations such as "always" and "never" are frequently heard. Beliefs such as "He/she should know what I want and need without me having to tell him/her, and if he/she loved me, he/she would do it," or "I should be able to control anything," frequently lead to unrealistic and dashed expectations and smoldering resentments or expressions of outright rage.

The counselor must identify such distortions and beliefs swiftly and confront them directly if marital counseling is to even get off the ground!

With regard to behaviors, the counselor needs to evaluate the quality of communication and conflict skills, along with the ability of each partner to make positive requests of the other and negotiate ways of fulfilling each other's wants and needs.

Communication skills. When the counselor assesses the communication skills present in the relationship, the focus is upon the following: the ability of each partner to clearly and effectively express thoughts and feelings in a responsible and personal way, using "I" statements, being brief, and focusing on one topic at a time; the ability to listen with empathy and confirm and reflect what was heard without judgments or critical tones; the ability to effectively use both verbal and non-verbal skills; the ability to make specific requests; the ability to give appropriate and well-timed feedback. Where these skills are present, shared or common meaning, true communication, can occur, and the work required to change various aspects of the relationship proceeds in a much smoother fashion.

Solving problems and making decisions. In this area, the marital counselor probes the ability of the couple to clearly define a problem, generate alternative solutions, and consider the potential positive and negative aspects of each of the proposals. Their ability to reach a decision regarding which proposal to pursue, to make an effective plan of action, carry it out and evaluate it is also considered. Where these skills are developed, the ability of the partners to become effective change-agents for themselves is greatly enhanced.

Managing conflict. As the pastoral counselor deals with the couple's conflicts, he/she assesses their ability to accept responsibility for their own feelings versus blaming the partner for what they feel. Questions such as the following are addressed: Can they identify the real issue and maintain a present orientation while discussing it, or must the past be dragged up? Can they put a conflict aside for a while and come back to it later, or must they "beat it into the ground"? Are they able to identify and affirm their points of commonality in the issue at hand, or do they just focus on the differences? Are their problem-solving processes effective, and can they celebrate when a conflict is resolved, or do they harbor unspoken resentments?

Many people have never learned to handle or manage conflict in a creative fashion, because they have learned that it is inherently "bad" or "sinful." On the contrary, conflict is potentially helpful in that it points up the need for relationship changes, and it is inevitable because people's needs change over time and rarely at the same time and pace as one's partner. It is not a question of whether or not conflict will be present in a relationship. It is just a question of whether it will be used creatively or destructively.

Sometimes when a counselor is assessing conflict and conflict utilization within the marital relationship, an internal sense emerges that the conflict goes beyond current or even recent issues or events, perhaps even beyond the marriage itself. In such cases, the vulnerability and rage appear to be so primitive that they defy all attempts at ventilation, bounding, reduction, resolution or reconciliation. In such a situation, short or long term individual therapy may be indicated to enable the individual to manage the vulnerability and the issues behind the conflict. If the therapist lacks the training for such in-depth work, or if it is believed that such individual work would unbalance the marital counseling too much, a referral to another clinician would be appropriate.

D. *The Original and Current Marital Contract*

Every marriage is based upon a contract, a set of expectations and agreements regarding the fulfillment of wants and needs in various areas of the relationship. Many of the agreements are "up front," conscious and verbally expressed. Others are conscious, but not verbalized, while still others are beyond conscious awareness. As the counselor facilitates discussion of each partner's wants, needs and expectations in the past and the present, various aspects of the original and current marital contract come into focus.

Clifford Sager (1976) has created a "Reminder List for Marriage Contract of Each Partner" which is a helpful tool to facilitate the exploration of a couple's marital contract. He suggests three major areas: categories based on expectations of marriage (e.g., to have a family); categories based on various biological and psychological needs (e.g., closeness-distance, dependence-independence); categories based on derivative or the externalized foci of other problems (e.g., interests, values, etc.). As each partner writes out a summary of what is expected and desired from the partner, along with an expression of what the writer is willing to give, and as these summaries are discussed, personal clarity usually increases, as does direct and specific expression of wants and needs, which increases the likelihood of them being met.

E. *The Extended Family and Life-Cycle Issues*

It has been said that we do not marry a person, but a family. How true! For better and for worse, a marital relationship does not begin or grow in a vacuum. Each of the partners is part of an extended family which has influenced and continues to influence how he/she relates to other people and to the world in general. Frequently, issues from generations long gone emerge in the current relationship. Old loyalty issues, emotional cut-offs, alliances, and expectations come back to haunt with a vengeance in the present, along with all of the beautiful messages and relational gifts and learnings passed from one generation to the next. Where each person fits into the extended family, and the impact of the extended family and the intergenerational messages and loyalties upon the current relationship, need to be assessed carefully. The positive dimensions need to be retained and affirmed, and attempts must be made to resolve those issues which are impacting negatively upon the here and now.

Assessment in this area also must include a look at where each partner and the couple itself fits into the individual and family life-cycle. Life stages and transitional points, such as "leaving the parents' world," "provisional adulthood," the "age-thirty transition," and the "mid-life transition" impact upon each individual and each relationship in different ways. Normal events such as the birth of a child or grandchild or embarking on a new and desired career can create pronounced positive and negative effects in a marriage, especially with the first occurrence of an event (e.g., the first child or grandchild). In addition, other common events such as a miscarriage or a job loss can impact in subtle and not so subtle ways upon individuals, couples and families. The counselor needs to assess how each partner and the relationship manages these life-cycle transitions, and to enable each person to appreciate the special issues and tasks associated with being at a particular point in the individual or family life-cycle.

Conclusion

A beginning pastoral marital therapist may initially be overwhelmed with the extensiveness and nature of the assessment which we are suggesting is required in order to do effective work. The more experienced pastoral counselor realizes how much information can be garnered from the answer received to a simple question. For example, in answering the question "What were your expectations of each other when you married, and how have they changed over the years?" a couple will generally give significant insights into his/her original and current marital contract.

But, even though an experienced clinician can gather, relate and integrate information, impressions and hypotheses more quickly than the neophyte, the fact remains that effective assessment requires a lot of energy and effort, a lot of careful thought and careful attention to both verbal and non-verbal cues. It is hard work! The "care of souls" is not an easy task, and if a pastor decides to develop this aspect of ministry, the price must be paid, or we run the risk of taking too lightly the task set before us. If that occurs, the counselor can contribute to the demise of a marital relationship, and that is a burden none of us desires to carry. Yet, if we take seriously the need to assess accurately and develop the skills necessary to do it effectively, the rewards are tremendous. With confidence, the pastoral marital counselor, working with the client couple, can create a treatment plan which can potentially lead to growth, change, increased wholeness, and genuine marital satisfaction and intimacy. The rewards then make the second task of the therapist in the counseling process well worth the effort: assess accurately.

For Further Reading

Beavers, R. *Successful Marriage.* New York: Norton, 1985. **Basic precepts for a successful marriage.**

Guerin, P.J., Jr., & Pendagast, E.G. "Evaluation of Family System and Genogram." In P.J. Guerin (ed.), *Family Therapy: Theory and Practice* (pp. 450–464). New York: Gardner Press, 1976. **Use of genograms for assessment.**

Levant, R.F. "Diagnostic Perspectives on the Family: Process, Structural and Historical Contextual Models." *American Journal of Family Therapy, 11*(2), 3–10, 1983.

Sluzki, C.E. "Marital Therapy from a Systems Theory Perspective." In T.J. Paolino and B.S. McCrady (eds.), *Marriage and Marital Therapy: Psychoanalytic, Behavioral and Systems Theory Perspectives* (pp. 366–394). New York: Brunner/Mazel, 1978. **Integrative book on differing approaches to marital therapy.**

Steinglass, P. "The Conceptualization of Marriage from a Systems Theory Perspective." In T.J. Paolino and B.S. McCrady (eds.), *Marriage and Marital Therapy: Psychoanalytic, Behavioral and Systems Theory Perspectives* (pp. 298–365). New York: Brunner/Mazel, 1978.

Chapter 5

The Tasks of the Therapist in the Counseling Process: Part II

In this second chapter addressing the tasks of the therapist in the counseling process, the focus is upon the need to develop flexible treatment plans, the need to develop and utilize a variety of intervention techniques, and the need to use oneself effectively. These tasks are addressed within a framework which highlights the stages of treatment and emphasizes the need for an integrated multi-theoretical approach to the treatment of marital problems.

1. Develop Flexible Treatment Plans

As the pastoral marital counselor or therapist is utilizing the ability to listen effectively and to assess accurately, the process of treatment is already well underway. Treatment of marital discord begins with the initial contact between the clients and the counselor, and within the framework of the local church it probably begins well before any official counseling session has occurred. As the parishioners perceive that the pastor is an open, caring, accepting, non-judgmental individual, and as they hear and see the good news through sermons and the life of the congregation, the pastor is viewed as an accessible person. As the sermons and the educational life of the church demonstrate a sensitivity to, and knowledge of, marital and relationship issues, he/she is perceived as a potentially accessible marital counselor. When the initial contact is made and the initial evaluation session is established, the "official" counseling process has begun.

As the pastoral counselor listens effectively and assesses accurately, interacting actively with the client couple, issues emerge, specific problem areas are identified, and the treatment team of pastoral counselor and client couple have the opportunity to begin to build a treatment plan.

We suggest to the trainees we supervise that they think in terms of a four to seven week evaluation period, and that they contract with each client couple for that period of time. During that time, the couple can be seen for one or two conjoint sessions, followed by one individual session for each partner, followed by three or four more conjoint sessions. During that initial period, the couple has the opportunity to settle in with the therapist and each has the opportunity to develop rapport with the other. Ventilation of stored up feelings frequently occurs early in the process, and this is frequently necessary to "take the pressure off" the marital situation. This occurs in both the conjoint and individual sessons, the latter being extremely helpful for each partner to gain the sense that he/she is being heard as a unique person by the counselor. The individual sessions also give the therapist the opportunity to see and hear how each partner relates when the other is not present. In such situations, the counselor is frequently surprised at the differences between the way an individual relates in a conjoint session and the individual sessions. Needless to say, this can provide the counselor and the client with potentially vital information for the conjoint sessions.

As the couple settles in with the counselor, and as rapport building and ventilation of built up pressure occurs, more energy and resources become available to identify the genuine issues and do an accurate assessment of the relationship, according to the guidelines of the previous section. Once the issues have been identified, the counselor and the couple can establish clear and specific goals which can then be worked toward as the therapeutic process continues.

For some couples, the four to seven sessions are sufficient. Once they have ventilated the pressure, dealt with hurt or angry feelings, identified the real issues and established clear goals, the latent or blocked relationship skills and strengths of the couple reemerge and they are able to continue the process of relationship change on their own, with only an occasional "check-up" with the pastoral marital counselor.

For other couples, the four to seven session evaluation period is just a beginning, and as the feelings are ventilated, the issues identified, and the goals established, there is a continuing realization that they do not as yet have the personal or relationship supports, re-sources or skills needed to attain their desired goals or maintain gains without the support and interventions of a counselor and an ongoing therapeutic relationship. For these couples, an extended therapeutic contract of another six to ten sessions is indicated, with a further re-view at the end of that period and each subsequent contract period.

The pastoral marital counselor who is willing or able to do only extremely short term work of four to seven sessions should indicate that clearly to each couple at the outset of the treatment process, so that if further work is needed beyond the initial contract period, the couple will be aware that a referral to another clinician will be made. This may still be a difficult transition for a couple to make, but it will be a lot easier for the transition to be made if the couple is prepared in advance rather than having it "dropped into their laps" at the last or next to last session of the initial contract period. (For a more de-tailed discussion of the referral process, see Chapter 7.)

It is important for the pastoral marital counselor to gain a com-mitment from the couple for the initial four to seven session evalua-tion period, and that sessions be held on a weekly basis. Without that commitment, many couples will terminate prematurely after the ini-tial ventilation of hurt and angry feelings occurs. The initial relief is frequently followed by a false sense of security as each partner feels better toward the other as they intentionally work to enhance the re-lationship at least to avoid further pain or gain a respite from further conflict. Although such initial positive feelings and beliefs about the relationship are a genuine aid in the therapeutic process, what they represent is not the same thing as integrated change, which can only take place over time and with continued reinforcement and practice. If the couple terminates prematurely, and the old issues reemerge several weeks or months later, they may be too embarrassed to return to counseling. Instead, they may then sit on the issues for an increas-ingly longer period of time, with growing resentments, pain, distance and hostility. When the situation finally explodes and one or both partners decide to seek counseling, it is often too late to effect positive change. We cannot overestimate the importance of establishing a suf-ficiently long initial evaluation period.

As is plainly evident, the evaluation period is also part of the treatment process, and is not just a preparation for it. During this phase of therapy, genuine and effective listening occurs and begins to be taught to, and practiced by, the couple. Ventilation occurs and defensiveness frequently diminishes, freeing resources and energy for more productive endeavors. Hope is instilled as empathy begins to develop, and as the counselor universalizes marital conflict and normalizes the occasional need for external support or counseling. Individual and relationship strengths are identified, along with areas of needed work. Goals are established and the couple contracts with each other and the therapist to do the work needed to attain the desired goals. Thus, commitment to the relationship is at least temporarily increased as the counselor requires and encourages commitment to the therapeutic process.

During the initial stage and all subsequent stages of therapy, the word "flexibility" must be paramount. Not all individuals and couples learn in the same way or in the same time frame. Every issue cannot be dealt with at the same time, and issue "A" may be of prime importance for one couple but of only minimal importance for another couple. Therefore, the pastoral marital counselor must be very careful not to impose his/her agenda upon any couple and to avoid the temptation to develop a "standardized" treatment plan that is used rather indiscriminately with each and every couple that comes in the door, whether they need it or not.

For example, we recommended the use of the PREPARE/ENRICH materials as part of the assessment process. Some counselors insist that the couple fill out the questionnaire before or at the first session, and proceed to use that instrument as the core of the counseling process. In our estimation, this is a misuse of a potentially helpful tool. For some couples the approach described above may be a somewhat helpful approach, but for others a period of dealing with hurt and angry feelings, of listening and developing empathy, of gaining a renewed sense that the partner cares, may have to precede any discussion of the more objective issues identified by such inventories.

Other counselors decide upon a specific set of skills they will "teach" to each couple, skills which perhaps most couples need to have in their repertoire in order to relate more effectively. But *when* such skills should be learned and *when* they can be utilized and integrated by the couple are just as important questions as "Do they need to learn this skill?" Here the issue of timing is just as crucial as the issue of what needs to be learned.

In all of the therapeutic process, flexibility is crucial. Therapy is an art form. Specific skills are required, but they must be used with varying degrees of intensity, shading and timing, sometimes directly, other times indirectly. Sometimes gentle reflection or empathic silence will accomplish more than an objective exploration of issues or an emphasis on skill development. At other times, to do anything else other than specific confrontation or specific skill training would be negligent on the part of the therapist. Sometimes a specific issue will be addressed appropriately, but in the midst of the discussion another issue will be triggered which requires immediate attention; yet, on other occasions, that "pressing" issue will need to be ignored because it is a resistive ploy to avoid dealing with the issue at hand.

Flexibility is the key! Flexible use of time, intensity, skills, support, confrontation, and so on, is necessary for effective marital counseling. As the counselor and the clients develop and move through the treatment plan, that word must remain constantly before them. Each person, each couple, is unique. Plastic overlays may be fine in the world of advertising, but in the world of counseling, flexibility is the key.

Of course, this is not to suggest that the pastoral marital counselor has a license to "fly by the seat of his/her pants." Flexibility, as it is used here, assumes an underlying firm theoretical foundation and extensive training and practice in a variety of therapeutic approaches. It is from such a broad and firm foundation, from an integrated multi-theoretical background, from a genuine eclectic base, that the confidence and competence required for professional flexibility emerges.

As was noted earlier, this idea of developing flexible treatment plans must characterize the entire process of marital counseling, from the initial evaluation period already discussed, all the way through to termination.

In the initial stage of therapy, some individuals and couples have magical expectations regarding the counselor, others are extremely dependent, while others are somewhat resistant to even being involved in the counseling process (e.g., the reluctant spouse who is there to please or "help" the partner). Still others are highly motivated and ready for interdependent relating, being "stuck" in just one particular area of their relationship. Each of these people and couples requires a different, flexible approach.

As the initial or beginning stage of therapy passes, the middle stage of therapy emerges, during which the process of hard work is intensified, as specific issues are focused upon in an in-depth way, and as specific homework assignments are given to the couple with the expectation that they will be accomplished in a committed and responsible fashion.

As the couple increases their skill development, resolves hurt and angry feelings, addresses extended family loyalty, entitlement and indebtedness issues, and in general proceeds toward the goals set during the evaluation and assessment phase, personal and relationship esteem generally build. There also emerges increased confidence that they can intervene positively on their own behalf, although they still may believe that they need the continuing support of the pastoral marital counselor and the therapeutic relationship. Gradually, the dependence upon the counselor is replaced by a growing sense of confidence, competence and independence.

This phase of therapy then gives way to the final phase of treatment, that of self-reliance and termination. Each partner and the couple gains an increasing sense that the changes they have made, and the skills they have developed, are not just "matters of chance," or the result of the therapist's magic or skill, but are the result of their honest reflection, empathic sharing and listening, hard work, disciplined practice and personal commitment to each other, the relationship and the therapeutic process. They believe in themselves, each other and the strength and viability of the marriage. They are able to objectively assess their strong points and areas of needed growth or continued weakness and vulnerability. They gain a sense that they can handle most of the issues that emerge between them, and that if further help is needed, they can seek it out for a short period of time. Competence, confidence, hope, trust, increased commitment, and interdependence characterize this phase of the therapeutic process.

It is important at this stage of the counseling process that the pastoral marital counselor be willing and able to "let go of the reins" whenever the couple is willing to take hold of them for themselves.

Sometimes the counselor's expressed faith in their abilities and continued confidence even if they initially have some difficult times will be the key in enabling the couple to move from the middle phase of treatment into the final phase. At the same time, the willingness to take control again for a brief period of time may also be necessary to enable the couple to get over a particuarly rough period and through a particularly difficult issue. If that is interpreted as a temporary measure and is treated rather lightly, the continued movement of the couple toward termination can continue.

Like the "little engine that could" in the children's story of the same name, the couple "thinks they can," but as they get near the top of the mountain, near the pinnacle, near their goal, they may feel increased pressure, fatigue, and renewed doubts. A little push over the top is frequently all that is needed to enable the couple to proudly proclaim, "I knew I could! I knew I could!"

When the therapeutic goals have almost been accomplished, and the couple's level of interdependent functioning has increased, the end of therapy is in sight. As the point of termination is clearly approaching, it is important that it be discussed several sessions in advance. Clients must have the assurance that they will generally determine when they have achieved their desired goals, and that therapy will terminate when they believe they are ready. Toward the end of the treatment process, it is generally helpful to put two weeks between appointments for one or two sessions, then four weeks between appointments for one or two sessions. This allows the couple to gain increased confidence that they can function well on their own and can work through difficult times between sessions. Throughout this period, the counselor needs to assure the clients that he/she is available for phone consultations or a special session if needed. In some cases it may even be desirable for the couple to call the therapist at an appointed time within the extended period between appointments just to "check-in." These supports serve as a necessary security system for the clients, enable them to have reduced anxiety, and thus facilitate the use of their energy and resources toward more productive ends.

When the actual day of termination arrives, the couple's process in therapy should be reviewed, along with each person's evaluation of what goals have been reached and what still remains to be done on their own. There should be a clear focus on what they have accomplished, how they have reached this point, and what each of them needs to do to maintain the gains already made and to move on to the pursuit of other goals. The pastoral marital counselor is, of course, an active participant in the process as well.

We frequently suggest that our clients establish a date three months later when they will sit down and discuss the "state of their marital union," how they are doing and feeling at that point in time. The following day they are then asked to call the counselor at a prearranged time, or come in for a quick check-up. Such a follow-up process generally insures that the couple will maintain at least some kind of a focus upon the relationship. If everything is going well, appropriate affirmations can be made. If some fine tuning still needs to be done, it can frequently be accomplished rather quickly and smoothly. If more serious issues have arisen or been resurrected, and are not being dealt with in a productive way, then some further counseling may be indicated, and may be accomplished before the relationship deteriorates too far.

It is clear from all of this that as the counseling process unfolds, develops and moves toward termination, the pastoral marital counselor must be constantly listening effectively and assessing accurately. This paves the way for the development of effective treatment plans with the client couple. These treatment plans must not be viewed as static entities that are set in stone, or inflexible plastic overlays that are imposed upon each and every couple in unimaginative ways. Rather, they must be viewed as flexible entities, constantly subject to review and revision, constantly being fine tuned and adjusted to meet the emerging needs of the individuals and the couple and the skills of the counselor. The third task of the therapist in the counseling process is abundantly clear and a vital necessity: develop flexible treatment plans.

2. Develop and Utilize a Variety of Intervention Techniques

In its infancy, the field of marital and family counseling or therapy was filled with people who were so busy developing their own ideas and techniques that there was little opportunity or time for the kind of cross-fertilization that leads to integrated theories and techniques. We would have expected that over the years, the Hegelian Dialectic would have become more operative than it has. We would have expected that those initial and various creative ideas or theses would have given rise to their opposites, or at least alternative ways of looking at the same phenomena, and that the interaction of those antitheses with the original theses would have given rise to a synthesis, which in time would become a new thesis, generating other antitheses and further syntheses. The net result should have been continued growth and development of the field, and the continued generation of new and creative ideas, theories and techniques. Sad to say, this has not occurred as fully and completely as it could have.

Instead of open inquiry and continued growth, change, modification and cross-fertilization in the field of marital and family counseling and therapy, we have seen too much myopic parochialism, too much lack of foresight and too many narrow, limited and provincial views. Second and third generation proponents of particular schools have often become even more rigid than their predecessors in espousing the virtues of their particular approach versus those of other schools of thought. Their training programs teach trainees a very narrow range of theory and techniques, with frequently only a token reference to other approaches. Proponents of genuine eclecticism are frequently dismissed as "shallow generalists."

It is our contention that such narrow-minded theoreticians and clinicians run the risk of doing significant harm to some of the couples who come to them for help. Their myopic parochialism blocks them from being able to do an effective, multi-dimensional assessment, and thus blocks them from being able to develop a broad-based treatment plan to meet the needs of the client couples.

We believe that pastoral marriage counselors or therapists need to disavow myopic parochialism, and to embrace a commitment to develop an integrated, multi-theoretical approach to their marital counseling. This will require a lot of hard work, for instead of being steeped in the literature, theories and techniques of one school, the clinician will have to become thoroughly familiar with the literature, theories, and techniques of a variety of schools. He/she will need to select the very best from each of the various schools and systems of thought, and then proceed to try to integrate it in a way that will enable him/her to assess and treat couples effectively. In other words, the pastoral marital therapist will have to become genuinely eclectic, and be continually open to revise the way individuals, couples and families are viewed and treated, as new and creative theories and techniques emerge.

The pastoral marital counselor is, in essence, challenged to become free from the shackles of the "law" of one particular school of therapy, and to embrace the "good news" which does not do away with the law, but in fact fulfills it. The good of the past must be retained, but the narrowness of myopic parochialism must be replaced with the heavy responsibility but joyous freedom which comes with the commitment to develop truly integrated, multi-theoretical approaches to marital counseling and therapy.

Such a commitment, and such an approach, requires that the pastoral counselor develop a wide variety of intervention techniques, based on sound theoretical bases. Psychodynamic techniques alone are insufficient, as are communication techniques, behavioral techniques, structural techniques, strategic techniques, and so forth, ad infinitum. The effective marital counselor needs to be able to draw on a variety of techniques to address the specific issues, needs and varying learning styles of the individuals and couples who come seeking help.

The purpose of this primer is not to give the reader a list of specific techniques which he/she can mix or match for use in the counseling process. To do so would require a volume of thousands of pages, and it would also perhaps give the impression that those techniques included are those we think to be the "best." If we did that, we would be contributing to the myopic parochialism we abhor. In addition, we do not believe that techniques should be learned in a cook-book fashion. Rather, they should emerge from the interaction of a sound theoretical base with the person of the therapist. As the various theories and techniques are studied, absorbed and integrated, the counselor is then able to "try out" various techniques and test how they "fit" with his/her value system, evolving theoretical orientation, comfort level and sense of self.

The pastoral marital therapist needs to also keep in mind that virtually anything that is done can be viewed as a technique. An appropriate smile, humor, a gentle touch on the shoulder at the end of the session, the PREPARE/ENRICH inventories, requesting that partners speak directly to each other, requesting that they reverse roles or change their physical seating arrangement, encouraging them to express feeling statements with the use of the introductory words "I feel . . . ," assigning non-genital pleasuring exercises in sex therapy, practicing brainstorming of alternative solutions to an identified problem, asking couples to write out their marital contract, etc., etc., etc., are all potentially effective techniques. In fact, the number and variety of techniques available for use by the pastoral marital counselor is limited only by the creativity of the therapist and the couple receiving help. Of course, personal comfort levels and value systems may influence which techniques are chosen to be used, and which are not, but the quantity and quality of available techniques is still limited only by the limits one places upon one's own creativity.

To be sure, there are specific techniques associated with certain schools of marital and family therapy, techniques with which the pastoral marital therapist should be familiar, and which should be practiced and utilized with appropriate theoretical understanding and supervision. As they are utilized, practiced over and over again, and integrated into the therapeutic orientation and style of the counselor, his/her armamentarium will increase over time. As this occurs, it will become increasingly likely that a greater variety of issues will be able to be dealt with in an increasingly greater variety of ways, which will increase the likelihood that more of the people seeking help from the pastoral counselor will be able to receive it!

We recommend that the reader desirous of being introduced to the theories and the variety of techniques of various schools or approaches to marital counseling and therapy read the following books:

N. S. Jacobson and A. S. Gurman (eds.), *Clinical Handbook of Marital Therapy*. New York: Guilford Press, 1986;

L. L'Abate and S. McHenry, *Handbook of Marital Interventions*. New York: Grune and Stratton, 1983;

G. P. Sholevar (ed.), *The Handbook of Marriage and Marital Therapy*. New York: SP Medical and Scientific Books, 1981;

C. Sager and B. Hunt, *Intimate Partners: Hidden Patterns in Love Relationships*. New York: McGraw-Hill, 1979;

D. L. Luecke, *The Relationship Manual: How To Diagnose, Build, or Enrich a Relationship.* Columbia, MD: The Relationship Institute, 1981.

The reading of these books will give the reader a solid, beginning foundation in the field of marital counseling or therapy.

It must be stated clearly, however, that the reading of several books is no substitute for an ongoing relationship with a supervisor with an integrated, multi-theoretical approach to marital counseling and therapy. In such a relationship, the theoretical base and skills of the developing therapist can be broadened and effectively honed. Where specific learning from a particular school's perspective is desired, in terms of theory and techniques, it is certainly appropriate to seek supervision or training in that particular approach from practitioners with demonstrated expertise in that area. There are many clinicians who have their foundation in a particular school, but are also quite open to, and knowledgeable of, other schools and approaches. They are quite able and willing to engage in constructive dialogue regarding "this approach versus that approach," and are quite respectful of the belief that "there is more than one way to skin a cat" effectively and ethically. Our only word of caution is to beware of myopic parochialism.

It may appear from all of this that the fourth task of the therapist in the counseling process is virtually a never-ending task. That is correct! The task of developing a variety of intervention techniques, if done within the framework of an integrated, multi-theoretical approach to pastoral marital counseling, is a continuing process of discovery, learning, practice and integration.

3. Use Oneself Effectively

The fifth task of the therapist in the counseling process involves the effective use of oneself. On the one hand, it is the most simple of the tasks. After all, it involves just being yourself. On the other hand, it is the most difficult of the tasks of the therapist, because it requires constant self-awareness and scrutiny and ruthless honesty with oneself.

The most important resource that the pastoral marital therapist brings to the counseling process is himself or herself. Each of us is our greatest resource, created by the Father, and co-partner with him in ministry. In the Son and the Spirit he is with us to the ends of the earth, and in the midst of our counseling ministry. It is, however, still us, as unique persons, who meet face to face with those individuals and couples who come to us with their hurts, pains, angers and betrayals, seeking our help to enable them to find reconciliation and intimacy in their marital relationship.

If we are to be able to enable marital partners to find those things with each other, we must surely be involved in the process of finding them within ourselves, with our Creator, and in the human relationships we experience in the world around us, married or not.

To use oneself effectively in the counseling process means that we know ourselves so well—our strengths, weaknesses and limitations; our feelings, thoughts and actions; our motivations, fears, and aspirations; our holiness and our sin—that we can differentiate ourselves and our own wants, needs and issues from those persons seeking our help. We are able to trust who we are, and to be sensitive to our own internal processes which are sometimes "hooked" while we are involved in the counseling process. When that occurs, we can accept responsibility for it as our own material or issue and maintain sufficient objectivity to continue the counseling process without "dumping" on our clients or "taking it out on them."

If we are using ourselves effectively, we can trust ourselves to use our joy, anger, fear and vulnerability in the counseling process. We can share our feelings and our perceptions, realizing that the latter are provisional tries which might turn out to be accurate, partially accurate or outright off the mark. And whichever way it turns out is okay, because we have no investment in being right, just in being helpful. We are also able to use empathy and touch appropriately, being secure with our sexuality, and, where appropriate, to use self-disclosure of particularly salient aspects of our own life, struggles and growth.

Effective use of the self requires that we acknowledge our own fallibility and sin, our own humanness. When we can do that, we face the reality that no matter how effective a marital counselor or therapist we might be, none of us is a guru. At best, we are persons who have been able to be of some help to others seeking growth, reconciliation or relief from pain. And, like all those who seek help from us, we have our own areas of vulnerability and needed work as well, the realization of which should help to keep us appropriately humble.

The pastoral marital counselor who effectively uses himself or herself has, or is actively working to attain, a solid self-identity and positive self-esteem. The recognition of imperfection or "blemishes" within oneself is accepted as part of the human condition, and what is pursued is a sense of emerging wholeness. It is this pursuit of wholeness and the belief that it is attainable which is transmitted in the counseling process to the clients with whom we work, and which provides the basis for hope and belief that creative change and growth can occur.

Through the entire counseling process there is the full realization on the part of the pastoral marital counselor that this is serious business. This does not mean that we cannot be playful, which indeed we at times must be if we are using our whole self creatively. Rather, it means that we take very seriously the responsibility to be as professional and ethical as possible, and the responsibility to obtain the appropriate training, supervision and continuing education needed to ensure that we are giving our best to our clients. It means that we must also take seriously the responsibility to take care of ourselves physically, emotionally, and spiritually, and to attend to the maintenance of our own intimate relationships, so that we can be as whole as possible as we help others. We must also remember, as we succeed and fail, scale the heights and plumb the depths, that if we are motivated by love, are appropriately responsible, and are fulfilling a genuine calling to pastoral ministry in our marital counseling, then God will continue to work in us, through us, and around us, if necessary, to effect wholeness (Romans 8:28).

One of the genuinely beautiful aspects of the Gospels is the fact that we catch a glimpse of One who was so comfortable with himself, so whole, that he could use all of himself effectively in whatever situation he found himself. Joy, commitment, tears, celebration, discretion, righteous indignation, anger, pain, fear, temptation, confrontation, gentleness, fatigue, intellect, etc., were all readily available for his use.

The fifth task of the therapist in the counseling process is to recognize oneself as the most important resource that is brought into the therapeutic relationship and to use oneself effectively to enable those seeking our help to find the wholeness they are searching for.

For Further Reading

American Psychiatric Association. *Diagnostic and Statistical Manual of Mental Disorders (DSM-III)*. Washington, D.C.: APA, 1980. **The basic work for diagnosing individual psychopathology.**

Anderson, D.A. *New Approaches to Family Pastoral Care*. Philadelphia: Fortress, 1980. **A life-cycle approach to family pastoral care in the church.**

Carter, E.A., and McGoldrick, M. *The Family Life Cycle*. New York: Gardner, 1980. **The basic work on the family life cycle.**

Hof, L., and Miller, W.R. *Marriage Enrichment: Philosophy, Process, and Program*. Bowie, Md.: Brady, 1981. **A comprehensive introduction to marriage enrichment, including its relationship to marital counseling and therapy.**

Miller, S., Nunnally, E.W., and Wackman, D.B. *Talking Together*. Minneapolis: Interpersonal Communication Programs, Inc. **A representative example of a basic couple's communication book.**

Sager, C. *Marriage Contracts and Couple Therapy*. New York: Brunner/Mazel, 1976. **The basic work on marital contracts or covenants and their place in couple therapy.**

Stuart, R.B. *Helping Couples Change*. New York: Guilford, 1980. **A Social learning approach to marital therapy.**

Chapter 6

Special Topics

There are a number of special aspects of the marital relationship and the field of marital therapy which have not been addressed elsewhere in this volume, but which are still due specific consideration. Among these, four specific areas need to be highlighted and discussed: individual therapy and marital issues; assisting a couple in the divorce process; counseling a remarried couple; working with sexual function and dysfunction.

1. Individual Therapy and Marital Issues

While there are some marital therapists and family theorists who insist that both partners must always be present in the therapeutic process, others suggest that mandatory inclusion of both spouses is often impractical and impossible in many situations. For instance, it is common for one partner to refuse treatment, or to insist that the partner go to therapy because he/she is in need of "help."

The logic behind the concept of reciprocal behavior in systems theory suggests that any one partner of a dyad contributes to, and therefore can change, the systemic pattern. Each partner's participation is needed to maintain a negative circular pattern, and therapy with one individual can lead to change in the contribution of the partner to the marital dysfunction. Of course, without the active involvement of both partners in the therapeutic process, there is a greater likelihood of emerging strong resistance to change, and thus an increased likelihood that the system will maintain its same old steady-state or functional equilibrium. In addition, without the active involvement of both partners, the possibilities of mutual, positive reinforcement are also potentially diminished. However, if one partner is truly motivated to change, but the other will not participate, it is better to work with the motivated partner than to not work with the difficulties at all.

The husband or wife experiencing some marital distress may come alone to the therapy sessions for many possible reasons. These reasons need to be ascertained and often confronted or reframed to put the therapy on a sound footing. For example, one spouse might come to therapy believing, reinforced by his/her partner, that he/she is the "problem" and totally responsible for the marital difficulty. Other times, the converse is true and the presenting partner will approach the therapist to gain support for his/her perspective that the other spouse is to blame. In such cases, as in most of the examples given below, it is usually important for the therapist to diligently ask the client to bring in his/her partner. However, this request should have some limitations. If the partner refuses to come, the spouse who wants to work on the marriage should be encouraged, for much can still be accomplished as the individual focuses on himself/herself and his/her positive and negative contributions to the marriage.

Continually asking the partner to come to therapy also raises an issue of power. An old rule of thumb states that the person with the least interest or emotional investment in a relationship has the most power. Therefore, the partner who resists therapy after a spouse strongly and sensitively requests the partner's presence is placed in too powerful a position. Such an imbalance of power can negatively affect both the individual client and/or a future therapeutic relationship with the absent spouse.

The husband or wife who is "sent" to therapy or feels the burden of responsibility needs some systemic understanding and personal insight into the marital dynamics. Such an individual can be taught to accept part of the responsibility for the marital difficulties but not all. Insights can be sought as to why the client accepts the fault or conversely projects it onto his/her partner. Dynamics underlying the taking of excessive responsibility are frequently found in family of origin issues and/or the marital relationship. In the family of origin the client might have been the identified patient, "bad child" of a destructive family system. Similarly, a specific early attribution, such as being told you are "stupid" or "incompetent" might never have been understood in historical context or differentiated, but simply adopted and carried into the adult years. Such early dynamics often enter the marriage in similar form, this time with the spouse, not the parents, stating that the client is "incompetent" or "stupid."

Another reason, among the many, that would account for a spouse coming to therapy alone is the desire to protect the perceived fragile ego of the partner. One of the possible early secret contracts of such a marriage would involve one spouse unconsciously communicating to the other, "I need you to take the responsibility for the problems in the marriage, such as with intimacy, and in return I will give you financial (or some other type) security." Often, the "responsible" client wants the therapist to perceive the protective pattern and relieve him/her of the burden of carrying it.

Perhaps the most common reason an individual and not a couple presents in therapy is that the spouse feels smothered and overwhelmed by his/her partner. Unable to maintain a positive sense of self within the marriage, such a person seeks out a therapist to help in the establishment or reestablishment of a sense of personal stability and emotional equilibrium. If a therapist is limited by his/her theoretical perspective and will only see the marital dyad, the insecure less dominant spouse is often the loser. In such a case the spouse will be asked to come into therapy before the partner can defend himself/herself appropriately. The entering spouse will then talk his/her partner out of coming to therapy, saying, "It is a waste of time." The weaker partner might not have the assertiveness to refuse the "request" to leave.

Still other individuals come to therapy because they are angry and frustrated with their spouse and do not know how to, or need assistance to, communicate constructively. Such individuals often come to therapy full of judgment and blame, hoping that the therapist will see the "wisdom" of their perspective and join the client in putting down the absent spouse. Of course, and as will be explained further, this approach in most cases would be highly unethical.

Whatever the dynamics of the individual coming to work on marital issues there are certain systemic principles that need to be followed in approaching the case. It is unethical to join with a client by being similarly judgmental of the absent spouse. The partner is not in the session to state his/her position and clearly the therapist is only listening to one-sided perceptions. The therapist who joins with the client in judgment of the spouse is inducted into the dysfunctional rules of the system and will be of no help.

Occasionally an individual will come to the pastor or lay leader and ask to be seen or share some information and add, "But don't tell my spouse." Within the context of the church this is often a very difficult and awkward situation for the pastor. As a general rule open communication should be encouraged. If a potential client insists on confidentiality from his/her spouse the safest course of action is to refer for counseling outside the context of the church. Questions of betrayal and loyalty and intense emotion can prohibit the pastoral care of the entire family if secrets are being held by the pastor.

As mentioned previously, in systemic thinking realistic acceptance of responsibility and self-knowledge is power for the individual. The client who accepts responsibility for all or none of the difficulties or strengths of the marriage is probably quite a powerless person within the context of the marriage. The role of the pastoral marital therapist is to assist the individual in understanding his/her "part" of the responsibility and encourage experimentation with more powerful and constructive behaviors designed to alleviate difficulties within the marriage. When a wife says, "My husband never pays any attention to me," the therapist needs to work with the client to help her understand what part she plays in setting up this lack of attention and how she reacts to it. The therapist cannot say something like, "It sounds as though your husband is not very thoughtful." When a husband states, "My wife is always critical and nothing satisfies her," the therapist can assist the client's learning his investment in his wife's rejection and what the secondary gains are. This type of systemic intervention will prevent the therapist from being triangulated into the relationship by the individual and taking sides. Furthermore, the therapist will not play a common role for pastors, that of being just the listening ear for the client's concerns. Such empathic listening can sometimes sufficiently calm the emotions of the spouse so that he/she will not feel the need to share the feelings directly with his/her partner. This can contribute to very long lasting individual therapy, high dependency on the therapist, and concurrent marital dissatisfaction in a dysfunctional status quo. It is easy and inappropriate for the therapist to be the better and more empathic listener consistently undermining the client's perceptions of his/her spouse as comparisons are made to the "wonderful" sensitivity of the therapist. If the pastoral therapist intervenes systemically, the client will have to take self-responsibility and more actively share feelings and perceptions with the absent partner.

An individual can affect the marital system and the therapist can work with this individual if systemic principles can be adhered to. The client is rarely a victim. Instead of being treated as such he/she should be instilled with power through insight or prescribed actions into the reciprocal nature of the marital problems. Once the client's contribution to the reciprocal pattern can be understood, the therapist can encourage the client to take the lead in effecting change. Reframing for the client, in such a situation, is often helpful. When the client states that he/she is "the problem" the therapist can remark that he/she has the courage and strength to try to understand the difficulties and seek change. The individual who comes to therapy can be the agent of reconciliation for the marriage.

If the spouse who has remained out of therapy for a number of sessions wants to participate, several issues should be considered. First, the spouse who has been in therapy must want his/her partner to be there and have discussed it with the therapist. The marital therapist is under no obligation to see whoever comes to the office and needs to keep control of who participates and who does not. Often, as mentioned, a partner will want to join the therapy to consciously or unconsciously undermine the process and return the relationship back to a former state. Second, the existing client needs to be prepared for the transition from individual therapy to marital. Often the spouse who is going from individual therapy to marital will experience feelings of loss or jealousy as the therapist now shares his/her attention, support, and confrontations with both partners. The therapist can help the client anticipate these different feelings and prepare him/her for the therapist's balanced approach. When such preparation is done the transition is often an easy and helpful one. Third, the partner who is entering therapy should be seen individually for at least one or two sessions in order for the therapist to get to know him/her and somewhat balance the time spent with each spouse. Fourth, in preparation for marital therapy, especially when one partner has been seen first, the pastoral counselor can speak with the couple about the importance of a balanced approach. Asking both clients to speak up if they are feeling aligned with or sided against is often helpful.

2. Assisting a Couple in the Divorce Process

For many pastoral therapists working with a divorcing couple, the first consideration is often a theological one. If the theological perspective of the pastoral therapist is that divorce is an unforgivable sin he/she should not be working in the field of marital therapy. The pastoral therapist who maintains that divorce is not an option for a couple coming to therapy can only minister to them in the context of bringing them together, or, as often happens, reconciling the couple to the status quo without consideration for how spiritually destructive the marriage is for either or both individuals. A reality is that many couples should not be married and were married for many of the wrong reasons in the first place. For example, an individual who marries to move away from parents, due to personal insecurity, because "everyone else is doing it," or out of an inability to live on one's own, begins a marriage in a very tenuous and unprepared way. If the pastor's position is that divorce is unspeakable, many such people will, in coming to the pastor for help, become full of guilt and lose any sense of the working of the Holy Spirit. The Spirit will be lost to the immense conflict and anxiety which can arise when a person wants to grow but the dynamics of the marital relationship prevent it. Furthermore, many couples who reject the pastor's judgmental attitude concerning divorce will not come for help to the church but go to a secular therapist. One healthy theological perspective for the pastoral marital therapist is to consider divorce as a sin, but it is a forgivable sin in certain destructive situations and can be accepted and reconciled as each partner works diligently to understand the mistakes he/she made and works to not repeat them. Forgiveness can be felt through the seeking of further individual insight and integration. With this perspective, divorce can be an option, after all else has failed, and the pastor can be a reconciling agent for the entire family assisting each member to start life anew with less internal conflict and pain. The pastoral therapist working with divorce can prevent it from becoming degrading and conflictual for the divorcing couple and devastating for the children.

If divorce is considered by the couple and therapist to be a fait accompli several considerations and interventions will help the couple and their children reconcile the past and feel healthier as individuals for the future.

The structure of therapy is extremely important. A general rule of thumb is that if a couple is divorcing the couple should meet together with the therapist for a relatively short period of time to discuss separating both physically and emotionally. A short period of time means no longer than five or six sessions. After this, in general, the therapy of choice is individual work with separate therapists. In individual therapy, work can consist of seeking increased differentiation and decreasing the attachments toward the marital partner. The pastoral therapist should generally not treat both spouses for a long period of time for fear that he/she will become a common link binding them together or be the conduit for communication. Seeing the couple for longer than five or six sessions will most likely turn into marital therapy and not divorce counseling. For example, the couple who spend multiple sessions criticizing and blaming each other under the pretense of working through feelings are probably using therapy to remain fused or emotionally bonded. The fears of separating and living alone can be so considerable that the couple will use therapy as a boxing ring to remain attached rather than deal with and work through the feelings of loss and separation. If such conflictual behavior, in the context of getting divorced, were to continue for several months the partners would become very tired and angry and less able to care for children or look hopefully into the future.

The children who witnessed such behavior would recognize consciouly or unconsciously that the emotional divorce was not taking place and that mom and dad are very much emotionally "wrapped up." It is in perceiving the parents' ambivalence that children will often begin acting out behavior in hopes of using their own power to keep the parents from following through on the divorce. A child finds power most often in ways which are destructive for the child, such as lower school grades, drugs, sex, etc., and which are designed to force the parents to pull together and concentrate on the child and not the marriage.

The therapeutic contract should be for short term marital work which facilitates separation and lessening of attachments within a context of respect, minimal conflict, and a very high regard for the health and the welfare of the children.

Apart from structure there are three other main considerations for the therapist working with divorcing couples. These are: (A) physical divorce, (B) emotional divorce, and (C) issues concerning the health of the children. All three will be discussed in hopes of fostering two specific dynamics, the couple's completing the divorce process so that each individual feels spiritually at peace and new relationships can be entered into freely without past attachments, and protection of the child's love and loyalty toward both parents.

In addition to the three main considerations discussed below, each spouse needs to enter the process of divorce with a firm knowledge of the laws relating to general divorce, custody of children, property settlement, etc., and be in consultation with a personal lawyer. In terms of dealing with the lawyer, several things can be suggested. Hopefully, many issues can be worked out between the couple before turning to the lawyer. However, anything that is negotiated by the couple should be looked at by each lawyer for basic comments on protection and fairness. Many negotiated settlements become very problematic in the future because a partner realizes that he/she did not have adequate information and actually was "shafted." Also the couple should be encouraged to maintain control of the divorce process by seeking out a lawyer who is sensitive to interpersonal issues, is supportive of a counseling process, and will be fair and not want to "get the partner for all he/she is worth."

Knowledgeable negotiating, control of the legal aspects of the divorce, and amicable discussion between spouses are crucial for the reconciliation process within each individual in the months and years to come. Angry and vengeful divorce is destructive for adults and often devastating for children.

Physical Divorce

Physical divorce means the actual separation of the two individuals, their finances and belongings. As a general rule, separation should mean exactly that. Couples may want to plan special events to keep a "family feeling" for the children, but this is rarely advisable. Separate birthdays and holidays with each parent will ensure that the children will completely mourn the divorce and experience special times without the friction and anxiety of having their parents together and more than likely being conflictual. The children need to remain loyal to both parents, and the "old" family tensions repeated at designated times will tend to force them to take sides. The reconstellation of the entire family also serves the couple's resistance to face the realities of the separation, mourn the divorce, and get on with their own lives.

The pastoral therapist should encourage the divorcing couple to find separate places to live and make the transition as smooth and orderly as can be arranged. It is important that each partner honor the privacy of each other's property by not coming without permission or not removing anything without discussion. Physical belongings should be separated within a reasonable period of time, and the division of property should not be made into a never ending process. Couples can remain bonded and conflictual when belongings are separated over an extended period of time. Finances should be negotiated once both partners have a complete knowledge of the assets and liabilities and not before. The goal is that much can be done by the couple without the lawyer, but with the lawyer's guidance, review, and "stamp of approval." The pastoral therapist should be on guard for any decision which will bind the couple in the future. Decisions such as having the couple renegotiate each month the amount of money one of them needs is destined to create continual conflict. Spelled out, concise, and written down agreements on finances, boundaries, visitation, etc., are most often suggested.

While the physical divorce might seem the most difficult, the emotional divorce usually takes longer.

Emotional Divorce

Couples who remain emotionally bonded long after the divorce often find it difficult to begin new, more constructive relationships. Children whose parents have not emotionally divorced can have many unresolved feelings. Examples of emotions which bond two individuals are love, caring, pity, anger, hatred, disgust, and rejection. Strong emotion between former spouses, whether it be positive or negative, will bond them together in some way. An important role for the pastoral therapist is to apply understanding and insight in the service of assisting the couple to understand the bonding and help them separate from each other.

In the few conjoint sessions at the beginning of the divorce process, the pastoral therapist needs to be quite forthright in preventing aggressive communication between the couple, unless it is deemed that the expression of such emotions will immediately lessen their power and facilitate further separation. They rarely do! The children need to be shielded, as much as possible, from such aggression. In such volatile situations, the pastoral therapist cannot be passive but needs to be strong and direct, undermining the process of projection of responsibility and blame. A sense of reconciling for the individual can most readily be reached when he/she begins to understand the systemic nature of the difficulties and accept his/her part of the responsibility. A divorcing person who feels that he/she is the entire fault or continually accepts no responsibility will often remain angry or justified, respectively, far past the physical divorce. It is then often difficult for each partner to develop new and more satisfying relationships.

Suggestions Concerning the Health of the Children

As mentioned previously, a main issue for the children of a divorcing couple is to remain loyal to, and in communication with, both parents. Children have a very primitive loyalty with both parents which needs to be protected. In order for this child to maintain parent loyalty and to be cared for appropriately, couples need to be taught and often forewarned to: (1) never put down or criticize the other parent in front of the children or with anyone; (2) facilitate the child's ability to see and call each parent; (3) never argue during the transfer of a child from one household to another; (4) to the degree possible try to make both homes truly a home, with toys, a child's place, friends, etc.; (5) remain as flexible as possible, keeping competition and jealousy from the former marriage outside of the relationship with the children. Obviously, with many angry and revengeful former spouses this level of cooperation is difficult to attain and the children almost always suffer. It is the role of the pastor to forcefully point out the consequences for the parents and the children if the anger and hostility continues unabated. Each member of the family's mental health is at stake!

In conclusion, divorce, in certain situations, can be appropriate and constructive, and possibly even necessary for the fostering of emotional and spiritual growth. In other situations, it is anything but that. Instead, it is a running from or refusal to look at oneself and the fears and hidden emotions which rule the personality. The process of divorce can be done in such a manner as to facilitate every member of the family's growth or it can be a destructive process which hurts all those who are involved. A pastoral marital therapist can and should work toward a healthy separation within a context of understanding and respect.

3. Counseling a Remarried Couple

Perhaps the most complicated of marital relationships exists when one or both partners have been previously married, and the remarried unit contains one or more children from a former marriage.

The issues and dynamics of remarriage often encompass the entire breadth of concepts of marital therapy. For example, the new partners often find it difficult to break ties with the former spouses. Guilt and anger for past "mistakes" can be brought into the new relationship. Remarried couples often find little time for romance, talking, or sharing privately, all of which are needed to consolidate and nurture the new marriage. Relationships with children are very complicated. Who loves whom? Who loves whom more than someone else? Are biological parent and child aligned against the stepparent? Often a new spouse will not have been a parent previously and with little preparation becomes one seemingly overnight. In such a case, the need for learning parenting skills can quickly become paramount. What is the relationship of the new spouse with the ex-spouse? How often do the children see the other parent and who pays what and for whom? The list of questions is endless and the issues are complex and often difficult for all parties. The pastoral marital therapist with some sensitivity to the above dynamics can intervene with a remarried couple in very concrete and basic ways to facilitate organization, increase understanding and foster respect each for the other.

Some areas to be addressed by the therapist are: (A) remarried couples and boundaries; (B) myths and expectations; (C) positive regard for the ex-spouse; (D) parenting; (E) building a new family history.

Remarried Couples and Boundaries

First and foremost, time for the couple to be alone needs to be protected. The demands of the blended family, children and schedules in particular, can overwhelm the couple and put marital relationship needs far down on the list of priorities. Time away together, dinners out, walks, and private conversations need to be protected by the couple and encouraged by the therapist. Such couple boundaries serve at least a twofold purpose: the new marriage can solidify, and a message can be given to the children that these parents are a team and work together, suggesting the stability of the new relationship, and the lack of need by the parents to be taken care of by the children.

Boundaries between the generations of family members are also crucial. Often, after the felt loss or absence of a mother or father, a child will begin to take over the role of the absent parent. Especially if the caretaking parent is needy, the child can become the comforter, helper, sleepmate, and general emotional support, roles generally reserved for a spouse. This is often destructive for the child and creates great confusion and conflict in a remarriage when a "new spouse" comes to take over the role of lover and comforter and the child is forced to return to being a child. Feelings of loss and/or alignments between a parent and a child against the new spouse can be consequences of lack of boundaries in the new marriage. Roles should be clearly defined as to who are the parents and who are the children. If a child is assigned the responsibility of taking care of younger siblings, he/she should be taught to give up the parental role when an adult comes home.

Physical boundaries between the generations are equally important. Parents should shut their bedroom door, keep children out of their bed, or from always being between them when they are showing affection. In general, the therapist and couple need to ask the question, "Are the roles of parent and child adequately defined and differentiated, and is there time for the remarried couple to spend together without interruption?"

Myths and Expectations

Many couples seeking to be remarried are filled with myths and unrealistic expectations as to what life will be like. One of the most recurring myths is that in a short time the family will look like the "Brady Bunch." This myth states that remarriage is fun, everyone loves everyone else, and all problems can be solved in a half hour. Other unrealistic expectations are that remarriage will be easy and will involve a smooth transition from the single life, or that the children should instantly love their new stepparent. This last expectation is especially damaging because there is no logical reason that a child should immediately love or trust a new "parent" and the expectation often results in the child hating the stepparent. Love and trust need to be nurtured within the relationship and will grow, in the best of cases, over time.

The important message for the marital therapist to convey is that remarriage is a wonderful opportunity to form a new family, but it takes work, patience, and, most of all, time and a good measure of coping.

Positive Regard for the Ex-Spouse

Divorce, in and of itself, need not be damaging for a child if, more than any other dynamics, two things occur. First, both parents must work through their anger, learn how to once again be respectful of the other and finish mourning the divorce. Second, each parent must communicate and demonstrate a positive regard for the former spouse and protect and support his/her relationship with the child. If both of these dynamics occur, a child will not have to suffer the real or felt loss of a parent or the torture of having to choose one parent over the other in a split loyalty.

Having positive regard means that one parent will not criticize the other in front of the children nor in any way triangulate the child into the middle of a conflictual relationship. Positive regard in a remarried couple needs to extend to all adults and possibly four sets of grandparents. Each child needs access to both of his or her parents without feeling anxiety or prejudice fed by one adult against another. Of course, this type of regard and thoughtfulness, putting the children's health in high priority, is unfortunately the exception and not the rule in many remarried families. The pastoral marital therapist must in no way be passive, but forthright in advocating each child's right to be loving and loyal to both parents without aligning with one parent against the other.

Without positive regard a number of destructive dynamics often ensue. A child can become deeply conflicted and depressed if he/she is told, "In order to love me you must hate your father/mother." For such a child, loving the new stepparent is often very difficult. In addition, a common scenario is that after a number of years of being taught to hate one parent and love the other, the child actually gets to know the estranged parent and discovers that everything that he/she was told negatively about the partner was either not true or exaggerated. In such a case, it is not unusual for the child to change alliances and become angry with the parent who did the negative "brainwashing."

Parenting

While there is no limit to material written on effective parenting, there are several considerations for parenting specifically within a remarried family. The pastoral therapist must realize that some adults are becoming parents for the first time and have not had the opportunity to develop parenting skills as most parents do, over time and through lots of trial and error. Training and discussion on parenting issues is an important aspect of therapy with remarried couples.

Suggestions for discussion in this area might be to ascertain what the stepparent will be called by the child. The name the child uses should not be mother or father, except in specific situations like the death of a parent when a child is very young. The first name of the stepparent is often used. The entire area of discipline and parent effectiveness needs careful consideration.

One of the most common themes in the remarried family is the absence of any functional authority to organize the family. Past guilt can affect present ability to be appropriately strict. One parent could fail to share information needed by another parent to be effective with a child. A child could be "protected" by the biological parent from the disciplining of the new partner. And in a variety of ways, one parent could undermine the effectiveness of another. The pastoral marital therapist must help the remarried couple to realize that effective discipline comes out of a nurturing and respectful relationship with the child, not from "on high," and that talking down to and being fearful of a child are destructive dynamics, and that for a constructive and healing stepparent and child relationship, time and constructive experiences together are needed perhaps more than anything else.

It is crucial that the remarried couple work together and present a united front while limiting the many and various ways that two parents can undermine each other. Protection of a child against the too authoritarian stepparent in most cases creates a very negative cycle which portrays the stepparent as too authoritarian and the real parent as weak and ineffective. A further crucial issue is to teach both parents to respond to the complexities of parenting issues and not to react. Reactions such as anger, violence, and yelling are signs of powerlessness, and although every family manifests some reactions, such should not be the major form of communication. Responsive language balances emotion and thought allowing an individual to directly express negative or positive emotions, i.e., "I feel hurt," "I don't like what you did," "I really respect your decision."

Parents in remarried families need to be taught to go slowly, limit initial expectations, and let the relationship develop gradually over time. Incidental testing and slow development of trust need to be normalized to thwart a need for major testing or continual crises by a child to gain distance.

Building a New History

The remarried family needs to establish a framework for building a family history. One way that families build such a framework is through tradition and ritual. The pastoral therapist can suggest that the family develop some new rituals around the holidays which are different from practices in the past. Examples are opening gifts at a certain time or eating certain foods at a specific meal. New rituals can be simple behaviors which can begin to solidify the group of people gathered in the same house into a working family. Rituals such as grace before dinner, family outings at specific times, family chats, etc., all can aid in the formation of the new family.

Recalling past events in a family can contribute significantly to the level of cohesiveness. Even if the family has only been formally together for one or two months, it is suggested that the therapist encourage the parents to recall the past by saying such things as "It was such a good time when we . . . " or "Remember a month ago when we . . . ?" These types of statements and consequent discussion start the process of building the family stories and sense of mutual investment.

In conclusion, the pastoral marital therapist must reinforce existing boundaries and support the establishment of boundaries, where there are none to protect the pivotal marital relationship and developing bond. Demythologizing and making unreal expectations more realistic are keys to formation of the family. Positive regard for the ex-spouse is important to protect the children from having to choose whom to love and whom not to love. Basic skills in parenting are often needed and welcomed by both parents but especially the parent who perhaps had no previous children. And new rituals and traditions are helpful in the formation of the new family.

4. Working with Sexual Function and Dysfunction

We live in a society that can be characterized as sexually traumatized, sexually secretive and sexually ignorant. On the one hand, sexuality is proclaimed to be an integral part of life, beautiful and even sacred; yet, on the other hand, it is used to sell everything from perfume to tires. Men, women and children have been sexually exploited. Churches and the clergy have frequently given parishioners conflicting messages: "Sex is dirty, rotten, sick and sinful; save it for marriage, when it will immediately become clean, healthy, beautiful and sacred!" Procreative aspects of sexuality have often been stressed to the exclusion or detriment of the pleasurable aspects, leaving a lot of confusion in the minds of many adults.

Secretiveness and ignorance have left people misinformed or unknowing about this important area of their lives—they have many unanswered questions, many misguided or downright wrong answers and beliefs, are confused about values and value-based decision making, cling to archaic myths (e.g., you cannot get pregnant while you are nursing), and do not even have a common, socially acceptable language with which to communicate about sex and sexuality issues.

It is no wonder that in such a society, sexual problems and dysfunctions are rampant. It has been estimated that over one half of all couples seeking marital counseling or therapy suffer from, or have experienced, a specific sexual dysfunction. When you add to those numbers the myriad couples who have difficulties with sexual intimacy because of misplaced or inappropriate guilt, shame or early trauma or sexual abuse, those who are simply uneducated or misinformed, those who simply need to develop their sexual skills (yes, effective sexual expression in marriage requires skill development), and those who need to learn to link sexuality and intimacy instead of leaving the two separate—when you add all of those together, the number of couples seeking marital counseling or therapy who also have significant sexual problems is probably a very large majority.

It is, therefore, imperative that the pastoral marital counselor or therapist be sufficiently comfortable with his/her own sexuality to be able to speak with a couple directly, openly, unashamedly and with love and compassion regarding their sexual life together. The therapist's use of words such as penis, vagina, intercourse and masturbation and specific sexual questions need to be free of anxiety and must communicate comfort with sexual issues. In the assessment stage, and throughout the therapeutic process, information regarding the quality of the couple's sexual experience and their level of satisfaction needs to be sought directly, and the couple needs to be enabled to develop effective communication and decision-making processes in this area of their life as in all other areas. Such information gathering is not inappropriate, intrusive, or voyeuristic on the part of the counselor/therapist if it is done as a routine and caring part of the assessment process, attempting to evaluate all dimensions of the couple's experience of intimacy in their relationship.

In order to gain insight into the sexual dynamics of the couple, the therapist needs to have knowledge of the sexual response cycle and healthy sexual functioning. Some couples will come into therapy complaining of a certain problem unrelated to sexuality because they are embarrassed or fearful of raising sexual difficulties with the pastor. The presenting problem is, therefore, a "red herring." If the pastoral therapist lacks knowledge or is fearful of asking straightforward questions regarding the sexual functioning of the couple, the hesitancy will be felt by all parties present and sexual concerns will not be raised or addressed in the direct manner necessary for their resolution.

Where the assessment process indicates intervention on the part of the therapist in the sexual area of the couple's relationship, several avenues of intervention are open to the therapist. Three of the following four treatment approaches—permission, information, behavioral suggestions—can be utilized by virtually any competent and caring marital therapist who has sufficient knowledge regarding individual and couple sexuality and intimacy, and is sufficently comfortable with his/her own sexuality that pertinent issues are not avoided or fraught with anxiety when discussed, and values are not imposed with rigid judgments or hostility upon the couple. The fourth approach—sex therapy—should be utilized only with special training and supervision.

Many couples simply need permission to enjoy their sexuality and permission to engage in or not engage in specific sexual behaviors. Open discussion of sexual issues with a representative of their faith can frequently lead to a genuine and personalized assessment of sexual values and behaviors, leading to increased freedom of individual and couple choice and affirmation in this area of life. Many "hang-ups" in the sexual life of individuals and couples are directly related to misunderstandings of religious teachings and faith principles on the subject of sexuality and sexual expression, poor teaching/preaching on the part of well-meaning, but misguided clerics. The giving of permission to explore and discuss values, to discuss sexual likes and dislikes, to decide what behaviors are personally pleasing or not pleasing, and so on, can help a couple to enhance their sexual life together.

Other couples also need specific and appropriate information. Because of our apparent societal values of sexual secretiveness and ignorance, many couples and individuals have not had the opportunity to receive high quality sexuality education. They may have read a book or two, but myths are frequently pervasive, and overlays of anxiety, guilt or shame can block the pursuit of, or incorporation and integration of, needed sexual information. The pastoral marital counselor/therapist can provide much information and a faith and value related discussion of the information through his/her own fund of knowledge and through the loan of high-quality educational materials (see the "For Further Reading" section of this chapter).

In addition to giving permission and supplying specific and appropriate information, the pastoral marital therapist can offer specific behavioral suggestions for the couple to utilize and enhance their sexual intimacy. The couple can be encouraged to practice specific sexual initiation and refusal skills; they can practice expressing likes and dislikes by reading a book such as *The Sex Atlas* and discussing it; they can learn to give and receive pleasure through non-genital pleasuring exercises; they can learn to create a conducive time and environment for experiencing sexual pleasure. The therapist can offer specific behavioral suggestions, help the couple to create or discover their own, and enable them to create a process for implementing, evaluating, modifying, and continuing the proposed behavioral changes. When such a process is developed, the likelihood of ongoing satisfaction and growth in the sexual area of marriage is greatly increased.

The fourth intervention approach when working with sexual function and dysfunction, namely, sex therapy, is highly specialized and should not be utilized without training and supervision by the pastoral marital therapist. To do effective sex therapy, the therapist must have a detailed knowledge of anatomy and physiology, the interaction of neurology and pharmacology, and the complex interaction of these with the intrapsychic, intergenerational and interpersonal dimensions of the individual, couple and family system and subsystems.

Issues such as performance anxiety, spectatoring, guilt, suppressed or repressed rage, intrapsychic or interpersonal blocks to the experiencing of pleasure, and deficits in social learning may all need to be addressed and overcome to enable the individual or couple to resolve the dysfunction and experience their potential in the sexual area of their life. An integrated, multi-modal approach is generally the most helpful, blending, where necessary, intrapsychic, behavioral (social learning and systematic desensitization), interpersonal and intergenerational approaches.

Sex therapy deals specifically with the resolution of psychosexual dysfunctions which include the following: (1) inhibited sexual desire; (2) inhibited sexual excitement (in males, erection problems; in females, lubrication-swelling response problems); (3) inhibited female orgasm; (4) inhibited male orgasm; (5) premature ejaculation; (6) functional dyspareunia, or painful genital pain; (7) functional vaginismus (involuntary spasms of the muscles of the vagina which interfere with or prevent intercourse); (8) ego-dystonic homosexuality.

A detailed discussion of the treatment of these sexual dysfunctions is beyond the scope of this chapter and the primer nature of this book. The three aforementioned intervention approaches are, of course, part of this more intensive approach as well. However, the complex interaction of physiology, psychology and marital systems theory in the etiology, maintenance and treatment of sexual dysfunctions requires specialized training and supervision for the therapist to be able to intervene effectively and ethically. When such training is not a part of the therapist's experience, a referral should be made to an appropriate clinician.

In many communities, certain medical doctors specializing in gynecology or urology have received training as sex therapists. More often, a marital therapist will have developed expertise in this area and will work hand-in-hand with an appropriate physician, forming a sex therapy team which can identify and treat the appropriate physiological, psychological, and interpersonal aspects of the sexual dysfunction from a genuine systems perspective.

Conclusion

In the practice of pastoral marital therapy a number of special topics need to be considered. It is not sufficient for the counselor to develop generalized therapeutic skills and apply them indiscriminately in all marital situations. An intervention or approach in one marital context might be very inappropriate in another.

Individual therapy has a definite place in a systems framework. Important is the pastoral marital therapist's insistence on working with his/her client's responsibility for the destructive marital dynamics and not allow sessions to be filled with judgment or blame. Individuals, instead of couples, come to therapy for a number of reasons. Accurate assessment is important.

In certain situations divorce is unavoidable. When conflict is deep seated and long standing and the workings of the Holy Spirit are lost in ignorance and conflict, divorce can mean a resumption of spirituality and growth for both partners. It also can be a grave mistake and a repetition of historical issues and undifferentiated aspects of the self. The pastoral marital therapist who is working with a divorcing couple must be sure to protect a systemic approach and not take sides. Both partners contributed to the marital break-up. The health of the children in large part is determined by the level of emotional enmeshment of the parents. All vitriolic behavior or asking a child to choose sides is very destructive.

The remarried couple is a growing population. The dynamics involved in working with them are complicated by differing loyalties, unclear areas of responsibility, destructive alignments, and often just the sheer numbers of people and schedules needing attention. The pastoral marital therapist will need to emphasize the establishment of appropriate boundaries, demythologizing unrealistic expectations, teaching the importance of a positive regard for the ex-spouse, parenting skills, and the assisting in the building of a new couple and family emotional history.

For Further Reading

Individual Therapy and Marital Issues

Berman, E.M. "The Individual Interview as a Treatment Technique in Conjoint Therapy." *American Journal of Family Therapy*, *10*(1), 27–37.

L'Abate, L. *Understanding and Helping the Individual in the Family*. New York: Grune & Stratton, 1976.

Assisting a Couple in the Divorce Process

Gardner, R. *The Parents' Book About Divorce.* New York: Doubleday, 1977. **Book for children and parents to share on divorce.**

Jewett, C. *Helping Children Cope with Separation and Loss.* Harvard, MA: Harvard Common Press, 1982.

Krantzler, M. *Creative Divorce.* New York: Signet, 1973. **Popular reading on divorce issues.**

Perry, P. and Lynch, M. *Mommy and Daddy Are Divorced.* New York: Dial, 1978. **Book for children and parents to share on divorce.**

Turner, N. "Divorce in Mid-Life." In Norman, W. & Scarmella, T. (eds.), *Mid-Life: Development and Clinical Issues.* New York: Brunner/Mazel, 1980.

Weiss, R. *Marital Separation.* New York: Basic, 1975. **General book on approaching divorce.**

Wheeler, Michael. *Divided Children: A Legal Guide for Divorcing Parents.* New York: Norton, 1980. **Legal implications for divorce.**

Counseling a Remarried Couple

Krementz, J. *How It Feels To Be Adopted.* New York: Knopf, 1982.

Lewis, H. *All About Families: The Second Time Around.* Atlanta: Peachtree, 1980. **Book for parents and children on remarriage.**

Sager, C., et al. *Treating the Remarried Family.* New York: Brunner/Mazel, 1983. **A general textbook on remarriage.**

Visher, E. and Viser, S. *Stepfamilies: A Guide to Working with Stepparents and Stepchildren.* New York: Brunner/Mazel, 1979. **A general textbook on remarriage.**

Sexual Function and Dysfunction

Barbach, L. *For Each Other: Sharing Sexual Intimacy.* New York: Anchor Books, 1983. **A practical, sensitive guide for increasing a couple's sexual intimacy.**

Haeberle, E.J. *The Sex Atlas.* New York: Seabury Press, 1978. **A well illustrated encyclopedia of sexuality, excellent for use by couple's to increase knowledge and stimulate discussion.**

Kaplan, H.S. *The New Sex Therapy.* New York: Brunner/Mazel, 1974. **A standard work on sex therapy, the active treatment of sexual dysfunctions.**

Kitzinger, S. *Woman's Experience of Sex.* New York: Penguin Books, 1983. **A guide to understanding female sexuality, and must reading for men as well as women.**

McCary, J. L. *McCary's Human Sexuality.* New York: D. Van Nostrand, 1978. **A standard textbook on human sexuality.**

Weeks, G.R. and Hof, L. (eds.). *Integrating Sex and Marital Therapy: A Clinical Guide.* New York: Brunner/Mazel, 1987. **The first book to integrate sex and marital therapy.**

Zilbergeld, B. *Male Sexuality.* Boston: Little, Brown and Co., 1978. **A guide to understanding male sexuality and the treatment of male sexual problems. Must reading for women as well as men.**

Chapter 7

Referral

Referral counseling is a type of short term therapy which includes joining or developing rapport with the client and building trust, stating personal and professional limitations, and helping the client to contact and work with the most appropriate professional who will address their particular needs. The ability to make a thoughtful and successful referral of an individual, couple or family to the best suited therapist is a crucial skill for pastors and pastoral therapists at every level of therapeutic experience and competence. Every pastor and pastoral therapist has professional limitations and personal strengths and weaknesses which could inhibit growth and insight in certain clients. No one can be an appropriate therapist for all people. The ability to refer and to recognize the importance of referral is a sign of self-understanding of personal limitation and general professional maturity.

The church for centuries has been known to be the organization within the community, perhaps more than any other, which will address the needs of people at a level of deep emotional need. Because of this, the church and its leaders are often the first resort, and sometimes the only resort, for individuals, couples, and families who are suffering and spiritually broken. If the pastoral therapist or lay leaders, due to possibly a lack of confidence in their own skills or a lack of general interest, turn such people away at this first request for counseling, many times no further help is sought, leaving people alone to deal with their pain. In other cases, potential clients turn to secular therapists and lose the spiritual dimension of the problem(s) and the hoped for reconciliation. The church can be a "gateway" for people who are experiencing difficulty, enabling them to enter into opportunities for insight and healing.

For these reasons, skills in making a sound referral are a necessity for all clergy and pastoral therapists. In any discussion on referral, the topics of whom to refer, therapist self-understanding, pastor

116

availability and relevant preaching, the referral network, referral dynamics, and referral techniques are particularly salient.

1. Whom To Refer

Individuals and couples seeking counseling from the pastoral therapist may be referred for a number of reasons: (1) as mentioned in Chapter 2 the client(s) might not be sufficiently boundaried to maintain confidentiality; (2) the client(s) may hold a position of importance within the administration of the church which would compromise the pastoral counselor's objectivity; (3) a couple's belief system might significantly conflict with that of the therapist's; (4) an individual or couple might present a specialized difficulty which is beyond the scope of the pastor's ability, i.e., need for medication, or serious psychopathology; (5) after the pastoral counselor and client(s) agree that marital therapy is complete, either or both individuals may want continued individual therapy. (It is most often best for the pastoral marital therapist to maintain his/her role as therapist for the couple and refer for individual work.)

2. Therapist Self-Understanding

The pastoral marital therapist may have considerable intellectual knowledge, even a collection of therapeutic skills and techniques, but his/her greatest gift and tool is the effective use of self with a client. If the pastoral marital therapist does not have a "sufficient" level of self-understanding, many inappropriate statements can be made, unhealthy relationships developed, and destructive dynamics created. At a minimum, "sufficient" means that the pastor or lay worker doing therapy can articulate publicly his/her limitations, describe the type of person or persons he/she finds difficult to relate to or work with in therapy, and be able to generally discuss personal and specific therapeutic strengths and weaknesses. The pastoral marital therapist should be able to define the role that therapy is going to play within the entire context of his/her ministry. Issues of apportioning time and discerning a comfort level with certain lengths of therapy need to be defined and discussed. Once the pastor or pastoral therapist understands his/her limitations and defines the role and priority that the practice of pastoral therapy is going to have in ministry, he/she should be able to communicate in such a way that people in the congregation and all potential clients understand these limitations and the definitions. With such clearly defined boundaries, people will find it easier to come to the pastor or lay leader for assistance because they will have a fairly good idea of what to expect.

3. Pastor Availability and Relevant Preaching

In order for the church to be truly a "gateway" and the pastor a "gatekeeper" for issues of healing and reconciliation, the church leaders must communicate in such a way that people feel accepted. Couples need to understand that if they bring their problems and "sins" to the church they will not be judged, but understood and effectively dealt with. It is always surprising to the authors that so many pastors and church leaders communicate to their congregants with so little empathy, understanding or insight into relationship dynamics, that sometimes people see them as the "last" people not the "first" to turn to when in need.

The pastoral marital therapist should be an open and non-judgmental person in order for parishioners and community people to seek their professional skills. He/she needs to be viewed as non-reactive, with good boundaries on his/her emotions. Effective listening skills, the ability to tolerate ambivalence, to not project black and white thinking, and to hold to standards of strict confidentiality, are all necessary skills and attributes for the referring pastor and pastoral counselor.

Many individuals and couples participate in church activities as well as Sunday morning worship. However, some people only know the pastor through worship and specifically through preaching. For this reason, the content and the manner of delivery of a sermon contribute greatly to whether a person in need will turn to the church for therapy. Preaching must, overall, be systemic in nature, using the systemic foundations in the scriptures. Pulling back judgment, the universality of sin, the importance of self-understanding, and responsibility for a problem laying on the shoulders of all participants are themes which speak to healing and reconciliation. Communicating these aspects of the scriptures will create a church environment in which people in crises or searching for new meaning will seek counseling.

Sermon delivery needs to be sensitive as well as reflective. The preacher should not come across as superior or inferior, but as a peer who is on his/her own journey. In a recent case, seen by both authors, a woman came for therapy because she was caught having an affair by her husband. Her husband told the pastor and she was ostracized by him and eventually other church members. No consideration was given to the husband's complicity in the affair and destructive marital dynamics. In fact, the husband had been violent within the marriage for a number of years and the wife's affair was an unsuccessful attempt to find some solace from the enmeshment and cruel treatment. If such a judgmental attitude is communicated by a pastor or the church leaders, few couples will seek out help within the church context.

As the pastor preaches about systemic understanding and "looking at the log in one's own eye," and as the spirit of the congregation moves toward acceptance and reconciliation, the church can become the first place that individuals, couples and families will turn to in times of need. As a redemptive community, the church can be the "gateway" and the pastor the "gatekeeper" in receiving people who need assistance, offerring them therapeutic expertise and/or appropriate referral.

4. A Referral Network

Before an adequate referral can be made, the pastor needs to get to know members of the helping professions within the community. A personal relationship which develops some mutual trust and understanding of the strengths and the weaknesses of both the pastor and the potential therapist who will receive referrals is needed. The pastor should know in what areas the referral source is particularly skilled or not skilled in working. Meeting with several psychiatrists for potential medication consults, with psychologists for referrals for specialized testing, with social workers, school counselors and other pastoral marital therapists can provide an extensive network of referral sources which the pastor can call upon when needed. It is best to begin looking for the above professionals within the church congregations of the community but not to be limited there. The label "Christian" psychiatrist or any type of counselor does not guarantee any level of expertise or even sensitivity to spiritual concerns.

A personal relationship with the referral source is very important for several other reasons. When the pastor or lay leader knows to whom he/she is referring a referral can be made with increased enthusiasm, and will communicate greater trust in the person's expertise. The referring pastor will also be more capable of matching up the right client with the appropriate therapist. Finally, a personal relationship and mutual trust are keys to ensure that the pastor can comfortably follow up on the progress of the case as well as keep informed as to the possibility of collaborative efforts.

5. Referral Dynamics

A common scenario for a couple who is experiencing marital difficulty is that some division and tension have been felt for a period of time before deciding to seek assistance. Eventually, the pain or the threat of consequences becomes so severe or tiring that the couple risks going beyond the bounds of their marriage or family to include an objective third party. If the pastor has communicated a gospel of reconciliation and forgiveness, such a couple will often initially turn to the church because of pre-existent trust and confidence levels. For some people, it is less of a stigma to go to the pastor than to the psychiatrist's office. Considering the pain and the courage it takes for a couple to come to the pastoral therapist in the first place, what happens if the pastor refers the couple to someone else without adequately listening to the couple and extending pastoral care? Both husband and wife could feel loss and rejection. Furthermore, the energy it took to come to therapy for help in the first place can dissipate after the seeming rejection, and the couple might decide to handle their difficulties on their own, which got them into trouble in the first place. Their management of the difficulty did not work prior to seeking help and probably will not again. However, the next time they might believe that there are less avenues for therapy that they will feel comfortable investigating.

Feelings of loss, betrayal, rejection, and abandonment are emotional dynamics in individuals and couples who are referred by the pastor too quickly or inappropriately. Furthermore, the beginning stages of a therapeutic alliance, when a couple shares history and background, requires a great deal of energy and vulnerability. If the couple is suddenly referred they often will not want to begin their story again.

In order to prevent feelings of loss and rejection a number of interventions can be made. The pastor or pastoral therapist can state his/her therapeutic limitations and the possibilities for referral at the beginning of therapy. If this is done from the outset, the topic of referral mentioned after several sessions will not come as a shock but as a predictable next step in the therapeutic process. For example, the pastor might say, "My skills are in communication and short-term behavioral work. Beyond this I refer to colleagues of mine who work more exclusively in the marital field. Why don't we work together for three or four sessions and at that time assess our progress? After these sessions we might agree to continue, to stop, or perhaps to consider a referral to someone who has more skills in the area of your concern." In this way, referral can be discussed as a possibility from the outset of a therapeutic relationship. This allows a couple to join with the pastoral therapist and most likely experience some relief of the marital distress, even if it be only in that a third party is expressing understanding. This enhanced trust and general relationship will make a referral by the pastor more creditable and acceptable.

The feelings of rejection or abandonment which can so easily be felt by a couple who is being referred can be further softened by the pastor or lay leader who discusses his/her ongoing role with the couple. The pastor can state that he/she will be there for pastoral support and encouragement as well as some follow-up with the couple at a later date. The suggestion that the couple make an extra effort to participate in church activities relates acceptance and provides community support.

In other examples, the client, not the pastoral therapist, might suggest that a referral to another therapist would be more helpful. It is crucial that the pastor not interpret this as a personal attack or rejection, but, instead, probe for client concerns and inquire as to the reasoning and then make the most appropriate referral.

The pastor, once the referral is made, should clearly define his/ her support for the couple. However, he/she should not be a "listening ear" for either individual. One of the most common forms of resistance to therapy is when either husband or wife finds an ally outside of the marriage to complain about the partner so that he/she will not have to take responsibility for the feelings in direct communication with the partner. In a similar fashion, a couple can return to the pastor to complain about what the therapist is saying. Sometimes this is legitimate criticism and a request for another referral needs to be considered. However, it is equally likely that going back to the pastor to complain and elicit support is an attempt to undermine the power of the therapist because of some truths that are being confronted and which are raising anxiety in the couple. The referring pastor or lay leader needs to be able to differentiate between a true complaint and resistance to growth. Probing questions into the meanings of the complaints are often helpful. It is always suggested that the couple be sent back to the therapist, if it be even for only one session, to deal directly and responsibly with their feelings, and not sidetrack them or diffuse them through the pastor.

6. Referral Techniques

As mentioned previously, the possibility of referral needs to be mentioned at the beginning of a counseling relationship. If the pastor or the client believes that a referral would be appropriate, a discussion should be held concerning specific wishes. Due consideration should be given to the age or gender of the desired therapist, as well as the need for him/her to have certain skills. Travel time and distance should be considered and time availability for both client and therapist understood. When these issues are not discussed, the pastor will often attempt to make a referral, and it will not work out. If the pastor does not follow-up immediately with both client and referral therapist, the problem can be compounded.

After the suggestion for a referral is brought up for the second time in therapy (the first time being in the initial session), an open and frank discussion among all parties is most likely to yield positive results. Couples will need an opportunity to raise questions concerning why a referral and to whom. The pastor should probe for unexpressed feelings that might undermine the referral after the couple leaves the office. If the couple agrees that the referral is a good idea, the pastor should ascertain the times that the couple could meet with the new therapist and tell the couple that he/she will be giving them a call within the next day. The pastor should then tell the client that he/she will call the new therapist to ascertain his/her availability at those times and general willingness to see the couple and will then contact them. Brief notes on the case need to be shared if the therapist communicates interest in seeing the couple. If the couple is aware of this, they are often relieved that they will not have to start sharing their story completely from the beginning.

Once all parties are in agreement, the couple should be given the telephone number of the therapist and asked to make contact and set up an appointment. It is important that the therapist, to whom they are being referred, not call the clients initially because it is the couple's motivation and determination to seek therapy which is so important for the first stages of the therapeutic process. If the therapist pursues the couple, it can quickly appear that the therapist is more interested in seeing the couple than the reverse. Within one or two more days, the pastor needs to follow-up with the couple, and possibly the therapist, to make sure that all connections have been made and a therapeutic alliance has begun.

As in all of pastoral ministry the referring pastor, lay leader, and pastoral marital therapist need to communicate continual support and appreciation of the client's desire to increase self-understanding and confront the difficulties being felt intrapsychically and in relationship with others. Being a sensitive referring pastor or therapist with a wide network of referral resources is a very legitimate ministerial role. Such a ministry will encourage many couples who would otherwise seek out secular therapists or no therapist at all to turn to the church for counseling or referral.

Chapter 8

Conclusion

If a practice of pastoral marital therapy is to heal and reconcile individuals and couples, it must begin with the overall health and integration of the pastoral counselor. There is a direct correlation between the maturity and level of differentiation of the pastoral therapist and the growth attained by couples in marital therapy.

Reconciliation is the cornerstone of pastoral marital therapy. Backed by the power of forgiveness of sins offerred by Jesus Christ, reconciliation offers the possibility for true integration of every aspect of personality and emotional experience. An individual moving toward a more reconciled position is able to limit projections onto a partner, be more compassionate of a spouse's failings, and ultimately examine himself/herself as the primary locus to effect change.

The Holy Spirit provides the healing energy for therapy. It continually pursues wholeness and greater truth and understanding within the individual. Much of the work of the pastoral marital therapist is to remove the blocks and diminish a couple's conflict so that the natural process of the Holy Spirit can continue.

Specifically blocking reconciliation and the work of the Holy Spirit are a number of marital dynamics aptly described in the New Testament. A lack of self-love leads to an inability to love one's neighbor. Judgment and blame result in projection of responsibility and reciprocal feelings of being judged. Feelings of superiority and inferiority prevent the vulnerability to be truly intimate with God or with a marital partner.

The definition and boundaries of the pastoral marital therapist's role are very important. Knowledge of personal and therapeutic limitations is a professional and ethical responsibility. Also in need of definition is the entire therapeutic milieu within the church. Confidentiality is the key concern. Not all clients who come for therapy within the church should be seen by the pastor. Besides taking into account the limitations of the pastor, the appropriateness and the boundaries of the presenting couple need to be considered. Clients who officiate on the ruling bodies of the church or who cannot maintain confidentiality should not be seen by the pastor, but referred. Referral should be a major aspect of the pastoral marital therapist's role.

In addition to personal growth a strong and in-depth conceptual background in a variety of systems approaches is necessary. Concepts such as differentiation, balance, self-responsibility, process and content, systemic questions, enactments, peer relationships, homeostasis, complementarity, merging the past and the present, boundaries, alignments, enmeshment and emotional cut-off, triangulation, legacy, introjection and projection, to name just a few, are basic for a marital systems approach. Such concepts need to not only be intellectually understood, and thoroughly integrated in therapeutic intervention, but as well be integrated into personal life style. The pastoral marital therapist will have difficulty trying to communicate or teach a concept which he/she is unable to personally apply.

A number of intrapersonal and interpersonal skills are needed in the practice of effective pastoral marital therapy. The specific tasks of the therapist are to: listen effectively, assess accurately, develop flexible treatment plans, develop and utilize a variety of intervention techniques, and use oneself effectively. The above tasks should evolve out of the therapeutic relationship and not be determined a priori. Many beginning pastoral marital therapists will lose flexibility and miss the emerging needs of the couples coming to therapy due to his/her own need to control, rigidly diagnose, or organize the session out of personal agenda instead of client need. All of the above tasks require continual supervision. The pastoral marital therapist should, on a regular basis, seek peer review and consultation.

Some treatment plans and intervention techniques are determined by the couple's specific situation. If an individual of a couple comes to therapy alone, the pastoral therapist must be careful, at least in part, to continue a systemic orientation. Judgment and blame should be redirected into insight and self-responsibility. The divorcing couple needs to be encouraged, first to seek understanding and insight, and second, if all else fails, to separate with as little enmeshment as possible. The children need to be protected from split loyalties. The remarried family needs to be understood in all of its

complexities. Above all, the remarried couple must learn to work together and effectively boundary their relationship from the needs
and alignments of the surrounding family.

Pastors and lay leaders do a major portion of all of the marital
therapy provided. It is an ethical responsibility and therapeutic necessity for the pastoral marital therapist to develop a sound and integrated theological, psychological, and systemic framework. Of
utmost importance is the pastoral therapist's sense of self and integration in order that he/she can effectively communicate, maintain
objectivity, confront accurately, and relate empathically. With such
an integration and conceptual foundation the pastoral marital therapist holds a very unique and powerful position bringing hope and
reconciliation to conflictual marriages and troubled individuals.